BLOOMFIELD.

EAST SURREY THEN AND NOW

Mark Davison

in association with
the Surrey Mirror Series

ARGUS BOOKS

Argus Books
Argus House
Boundary Way
Hemel Hempstead
Herts HP2 7ST
England

First published by Argus Books 1992

ISBN 1 85486 036 4

Phototypesetting by The Studio, Exeter.
Printed and bound in Great Britain by Clays Ltd., St. Ives plc, Bungay.

Foreword

This is where we live, in the midst of beautiful countryside, yet close to London, to motorways and airports.

It has always been an area of variety – of scenery, natural resources, buildings and, most important, people. Over the centuries they have lived their lives, built their homes and their churches, established their industries and businesses. All these have left their individual marks.

Visitors to Reigate Priory Museum take most interest in our exhibitions with a local theme, so I am sure that the photographs, the anecdotes and the information presented in this special *Surrey Mirror* publication will interest us all – and, perhaps, set us thinking about what we are contributing to the future.

Audrey J Ward
Museum Organiser
Reigate Priory Museum

About the author

Mark Davison is deputy editor of the Surrey Mirror Series and for five years compiled the popular weekly 'Yesteryear' column. Prior to this, he ran a series of articles on local history in both the Kingston Borough News and the Banstead Herald.

Apart from delving into the county's past, he is interested in weather and climate and has co-written two books about the Great Storm of October 1987 – *Surrey In The Hurricane* and *London's Hurricane*. He then produced a book of pictures and stories about severe weather in Surrey over the past 100 years, called simply, *The Surrey Weather Book*. This led him to join forces with co-authors Ian Currie and Bob Ogley to compile the Sussex, Kent and Essex Weather Books.

Acknowledgements

In addition to the many readers of 'Yesteryear' in the *Surrey Mirror* series, whose contributions have enabled this book to be compiled, the following are especially thanked:

The Bourne Society
John Roper
Derek Moore, chairman of the Bletchingley Conservation and Historical Society
Charles Reason
Jack Sales
David Watkins
Peter Gardner
Bob Heron
Neil McGinn
John Huxtable
Valerie Attwater
Directors, Surrey and South London Newspapers.

Bibliography

Horley – Pageant of a Wealden Parish. Chouler
Branch Lines to Tunbridge Wells from Oxted, Lewes and Polegate. Vic Mitchell and Keith Smith (Middleton Press).
Reigate: Its Story Through The Ages. Wilfrid Hooper (Kohler and Coombes).
The Doctor's Tale. Lawrence Dulake. (Lawrence Dulake).
Felbridge School.
Charlwood and Horley Cottage Hospitals 1873–1983. Compiled by Mrs Jean Shelley, Mrs Joyce Lucas and Dr A. G. T. Brown.
A Century At Caterham 1884–1984. Ernest de C. Blomfield (Kier and Reid).
Who's Who In Surrey (Ebenezer Baylis and Sons Ltd (1936)).
Towns With Character. Arthur Hutchinson (A. J. French, Chichester 1985).
Then and Now – The Changing Scene of Surrey Life in Caterham, Coulsdon and Warlingham areas. The Bourne Society.

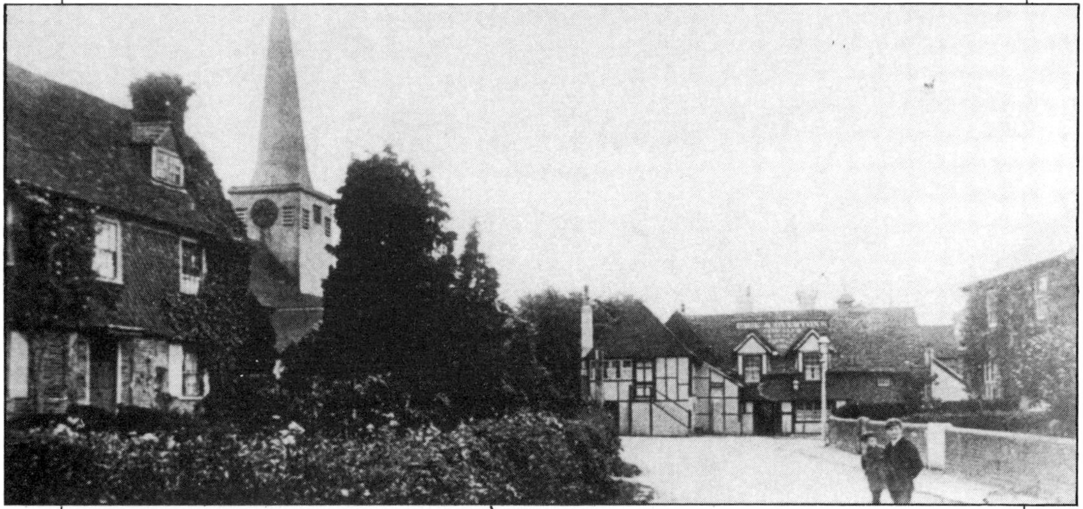

Little has changed in this comparison of old and new. The picture above shows the Six Bells public house in Church Road, Horley, some eight decades ago.

Today, only a modern lamp-post detracts from the rural charm of those bygone days.

It is said that the services held in St Bartholomew's Church centuries ago were so long that there was a great demand for a nearby place to partake of refreshments. A document of 1304 refers to an 'eating house' at this spot which was surrounded by land belonging to 'Longbragge' which later became Longbridge.

Towards the end of the 14th century, the inn was increased in size to cater for the people attending the monthly courts held in the Court Lodge Manor. A sign for the Six Bells was first put up in 1393 when King Richard II passed a law — ''Whoever shall brew ale with intention of selling it shall put up a sign or else forefeit his ale!''

Today, the Six Bells is a popular venue for hundreds of young Horley residents. In 1988, crowds celebrated a new extension, listening to live music provided by local artists.

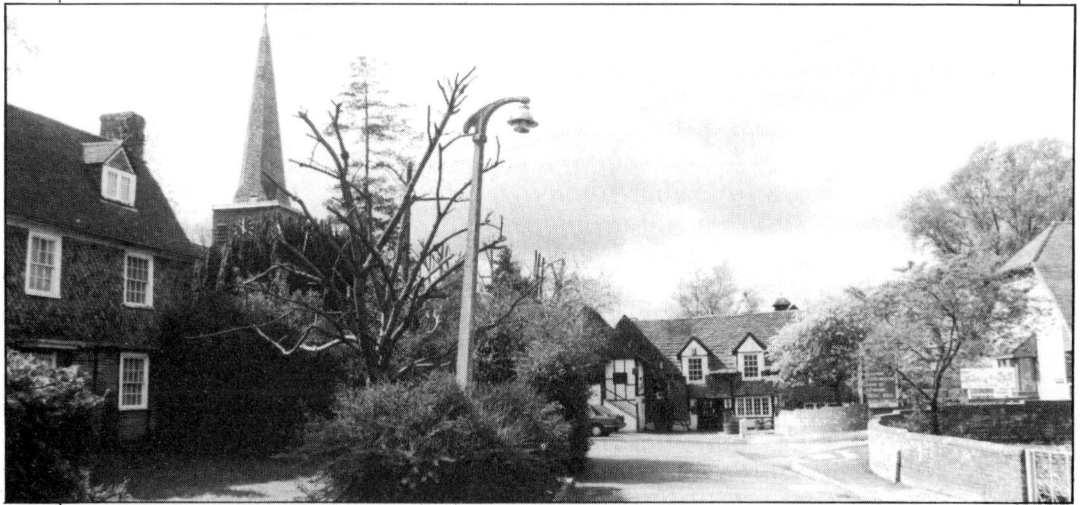

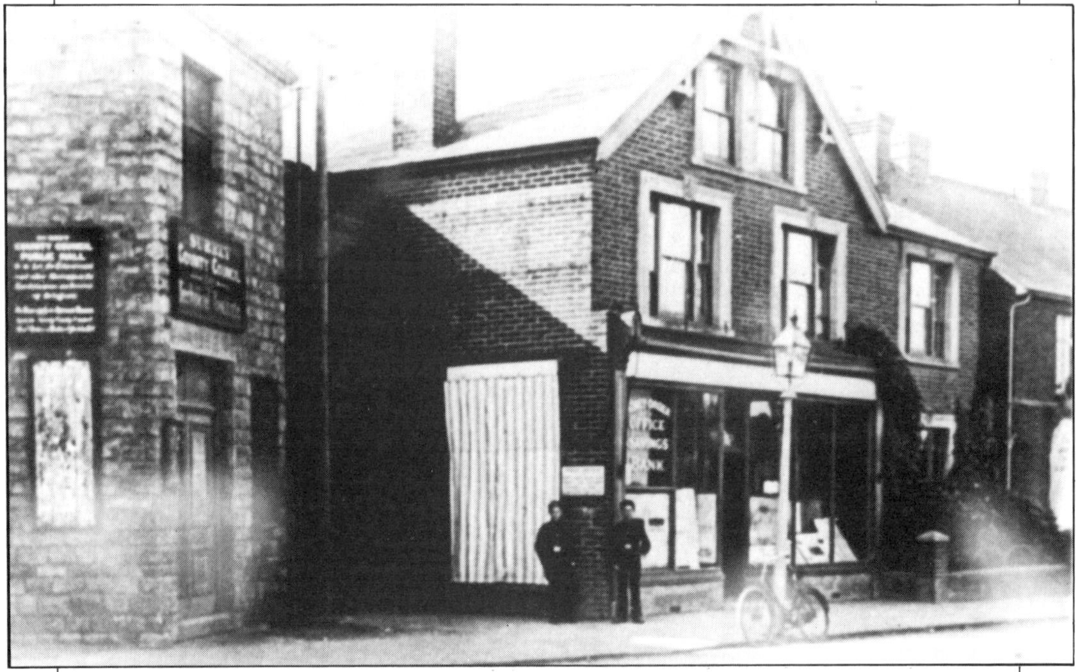

The old post office in Horley stood at the corner of High Street and Yattendon Road, opposite the railway footbridge.

What excitement there was when decorated trains passed by celebrating such battles as Trafalgar and Waterloo!

Today, the building is used for selling motor accessories.

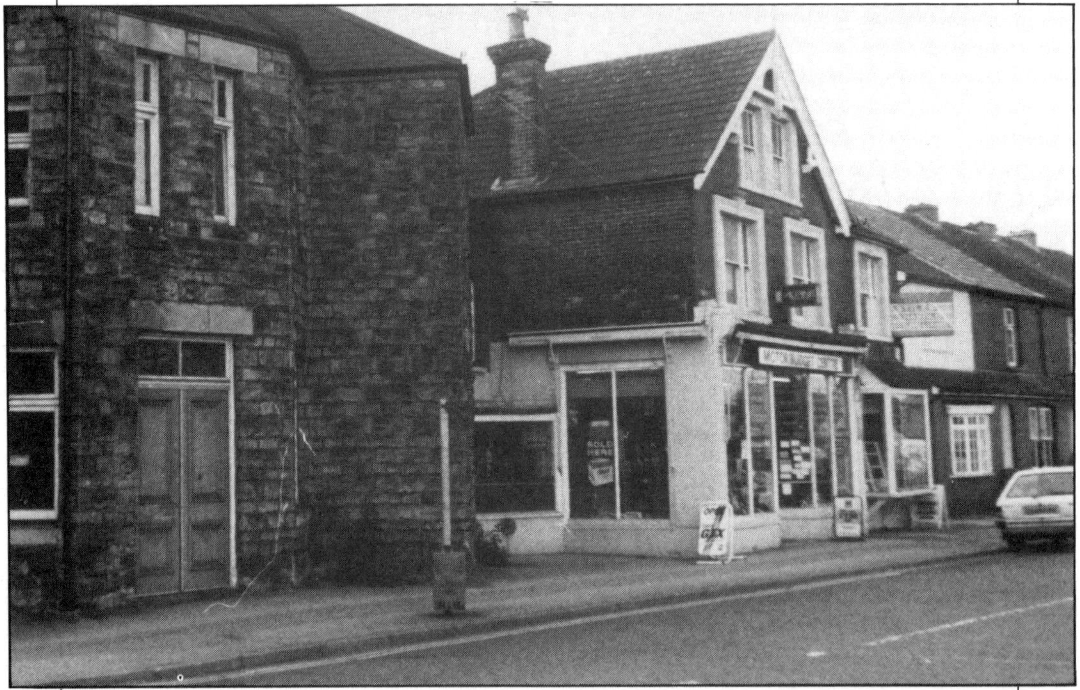

Horley Brewery is thought to have been established by Messrs Newnham and Piper who sold it to Francis Albert Piper and Co in 1867. In about 1885 it was sold to Charles Dagnall and Co and, in 1890 it became the old Hornchurch Brewery Co. Ltd, Charles Dagnall being the managing director.

By this time, the brewery buildings had been largely rebuilt and considerably extended and the brewery house erected. The following year it was resold and the name appears to have remained unchanged. The new owner was George Brown whose grandson, A. O. Brown, lives in the town today and is deeply interested in local history. George Brown was once the landlord of The Chequers public house, which dates back to at least 1537, and was once known as 'Bolters'.

In 1894 Horley Brewery was sold to Yovell and Elkin who in turn passed it to Croydon brewers Page and Overton in 1903. They carried on business at Horley until 1917. In 1902 the brewery had agencies as far away as London, Burgess Hill, Oxted and Rusper.

In the parlour of the brewery house was a piano which, as a young girl, Mrs E. Mitchell used to play. Her uncle, John Woodman worked there in Edwardian times. Mrs Mitchell was still living in Lee Street as a nonogenarian.

Water for the brewery was supplied by an artesian well on the premises.

The Horley Brewery staff in about 1900. Third from the right in the top row is brewer Arthur Brown.

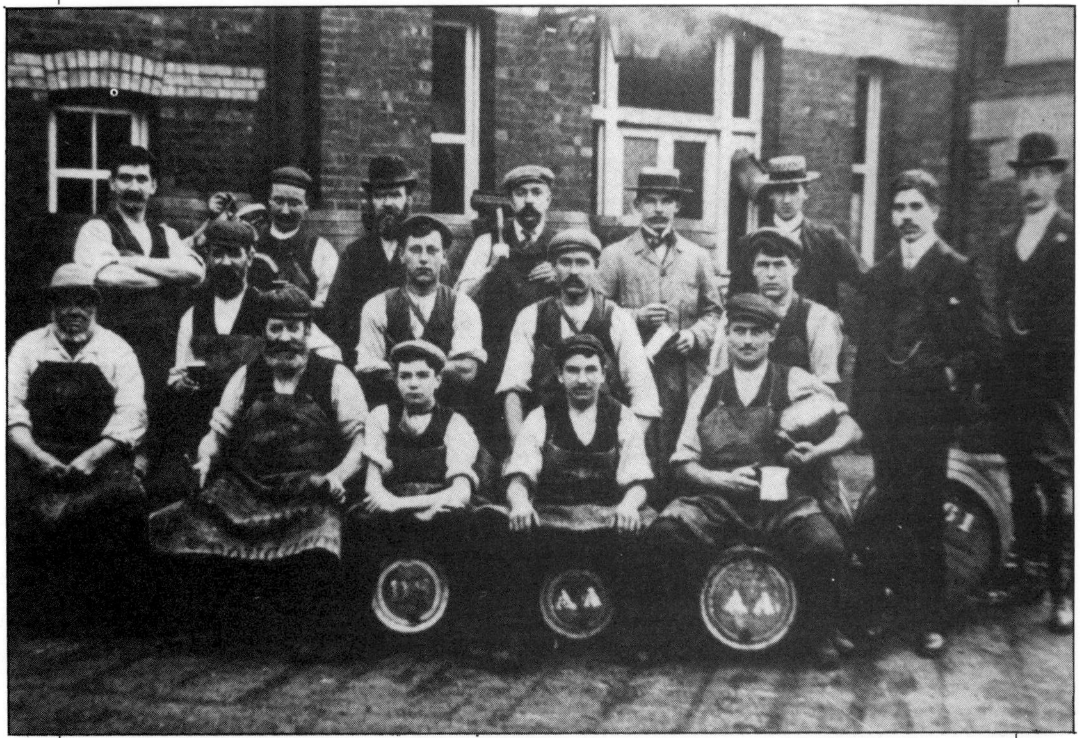

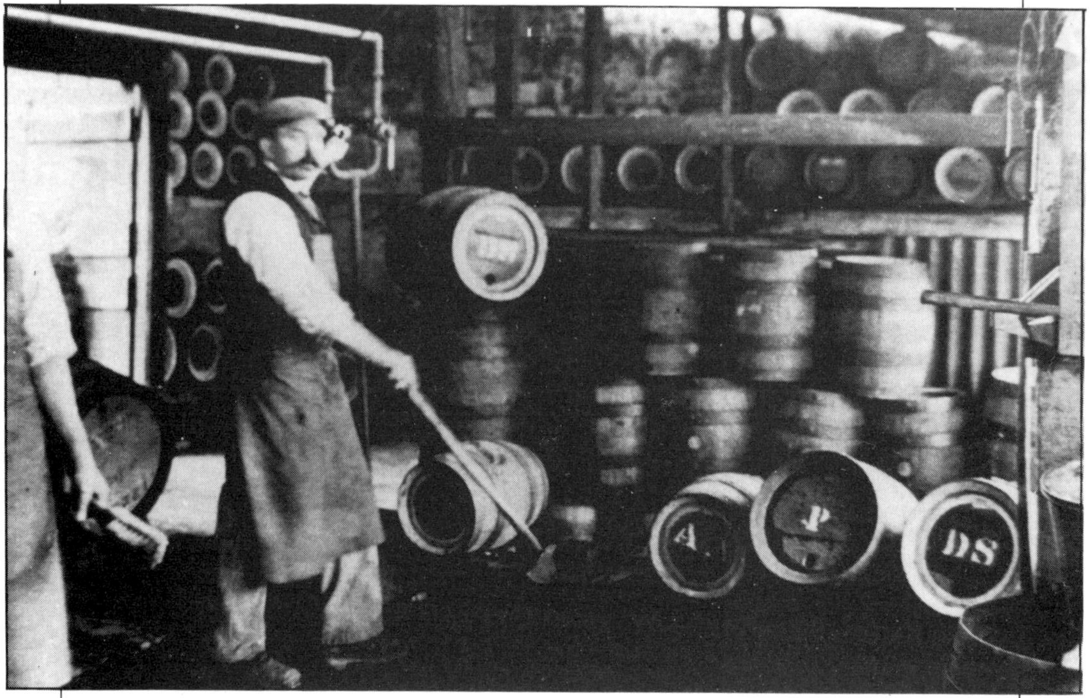

Keeping an eye on the storage of barrels.

Getting the supplies out on the road.

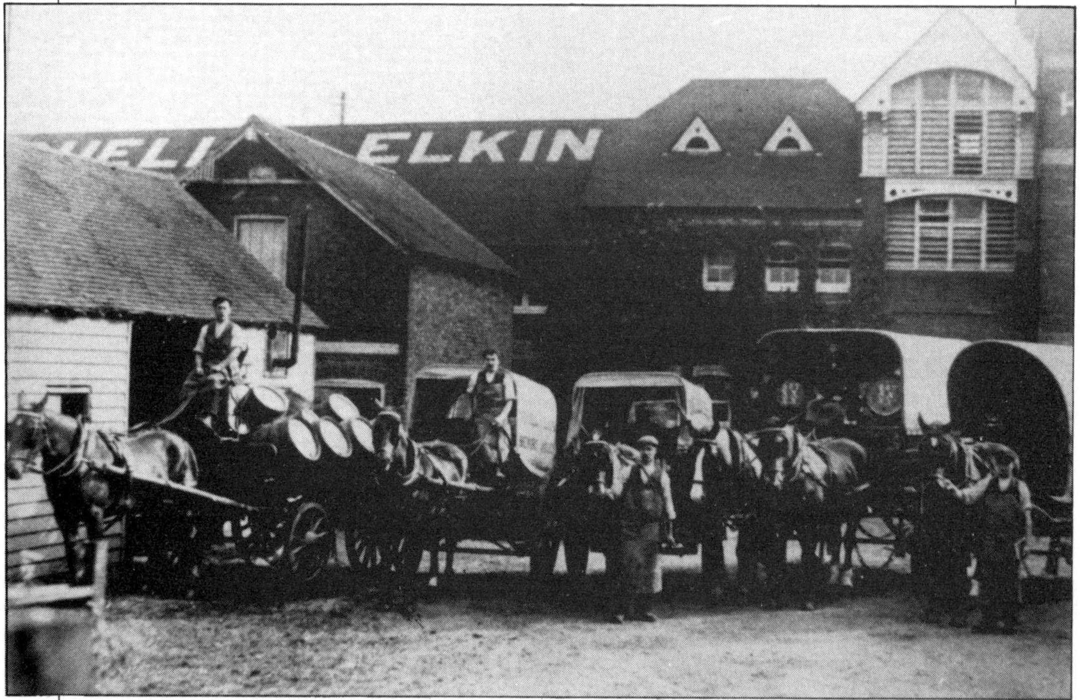

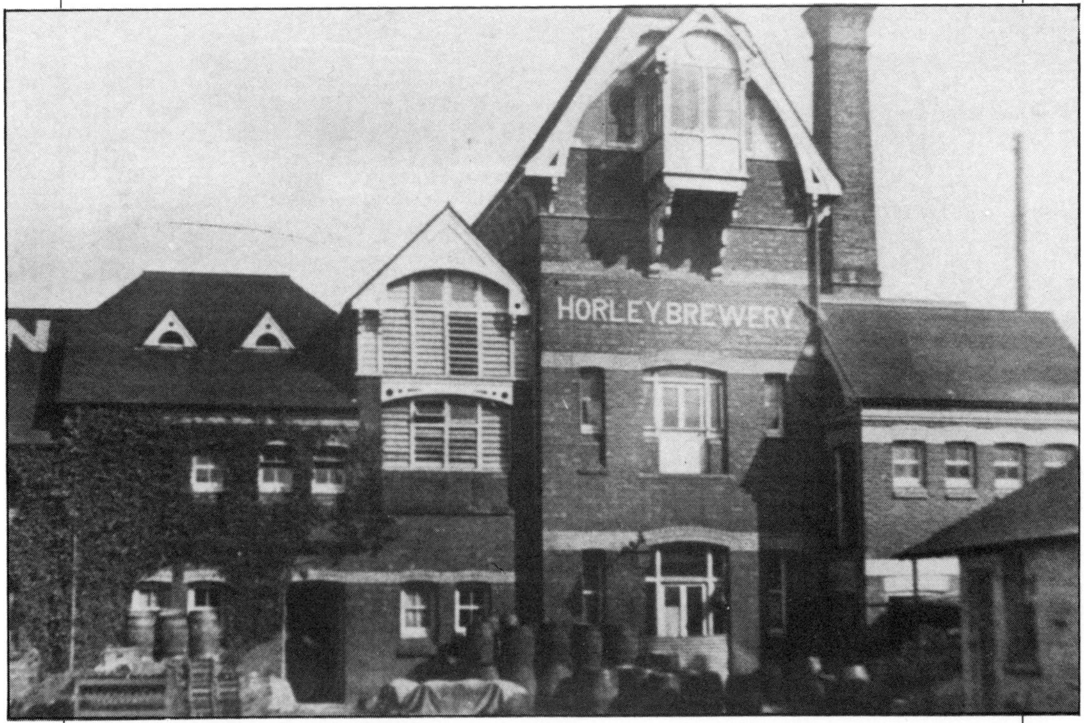

The mid-Victorian brewery building.

Children at Lumley Road school, Horley, in the 1930s.

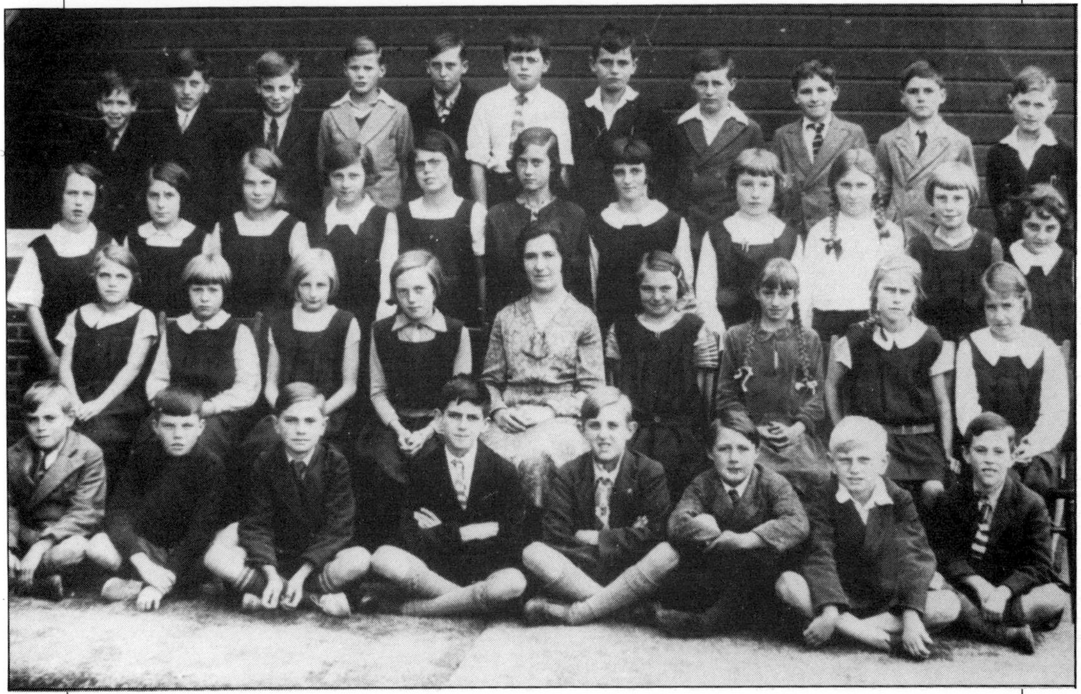

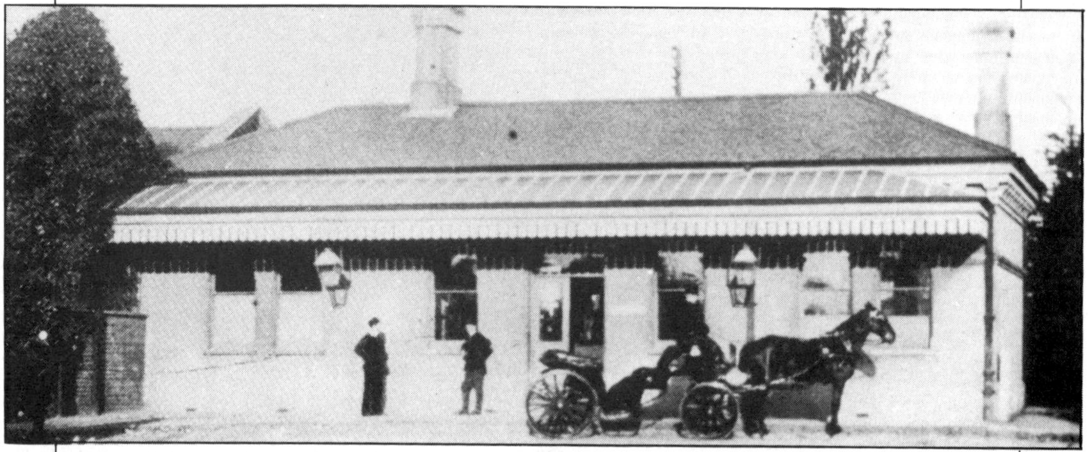

The old Horley Station in Station Road which was moved to its present position in 1905.

When the original Horley Station was built in 1841 on the site of today's garden centre in Station Road, Horley was a very small village with just one shop which stood next to The Chequers inn. But, by the 1890s, the popularity of the town had grown. Being within an easy train ride to London or Brighton, and being set in beautiful surroundings, the little Surrey village proved to be a magnet for developers.

An area around Lumley Road was chosen for house building, and by 1901 – the year of Queen Victoria's death – the population of Horley had risen to 4,111. In 1905, the station was re-sited further south to allow for expansion.

The late Mr Cecil Johnson, who died in 1982, wrote down his memories of the old station in the book *Horley – Pageant of a Wealden Parish* by W. H. Chouler. He said: "For such a small place, the station was large and of a striking design, especially the 'up' platform. This consisted of a long platform with a colonnade of brick pillars which supported the covered roof. These pillars were mostly covered by ivy or virginia creeper.

"The stationmaster during the early nineties was named Holdway. He had a good portly figure, auburn hair and a fine gingery moustache. He looked very smart in his gold braided frock coat and top hat."

On cold winter mornings, the porters put long brass foot warmers in the compartments for the passengers' comfort.

The old station site is now used as a garden centre.

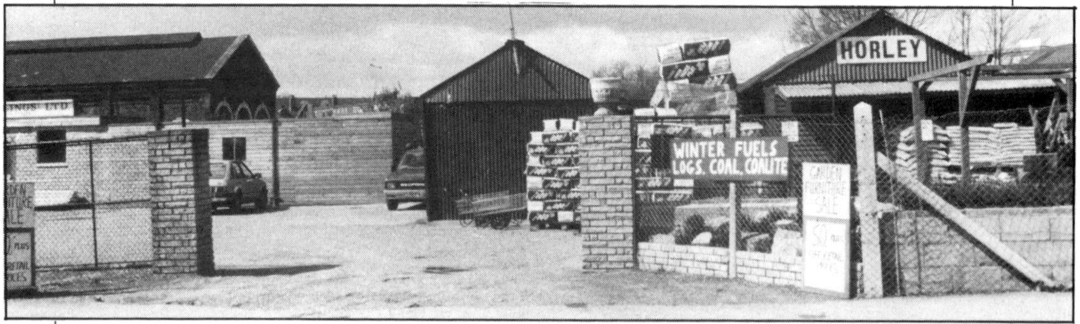

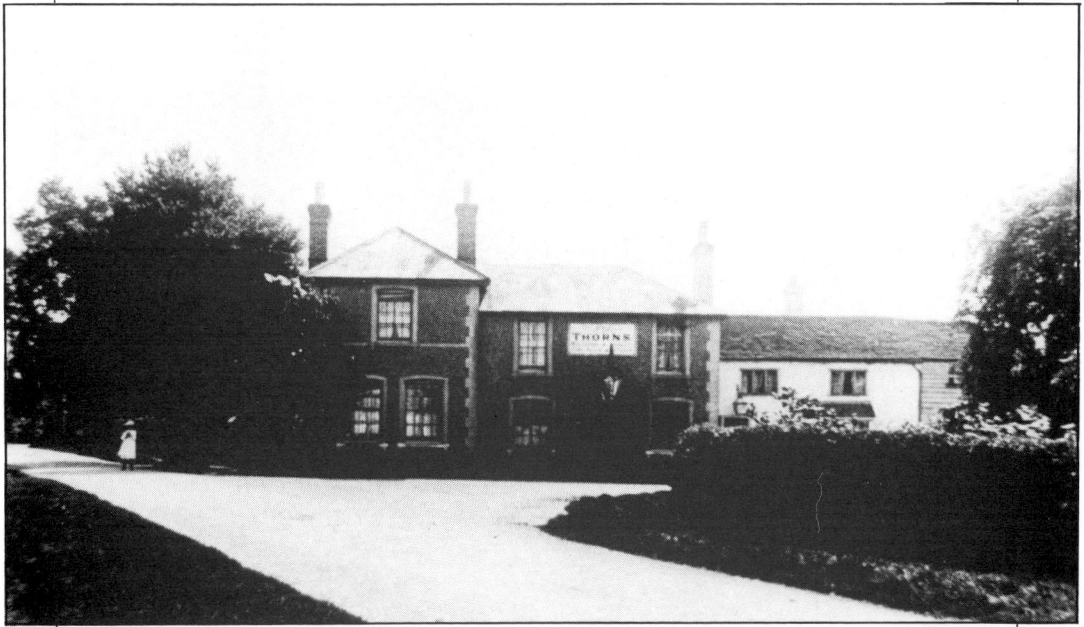

Today, the Game Bird public house stands at the junction of the A23 and Victoria Road in Horley, and is a popular haunt of the town's young people. It is only in recent years that it has taken on this name, and many Horley people still call it by its former title of The Thorns.

The old picture shows how it looked at the turn of the century. Note, there is no sign advertising flights to New York for £249 as displayed in the bus shelter in the new picture!

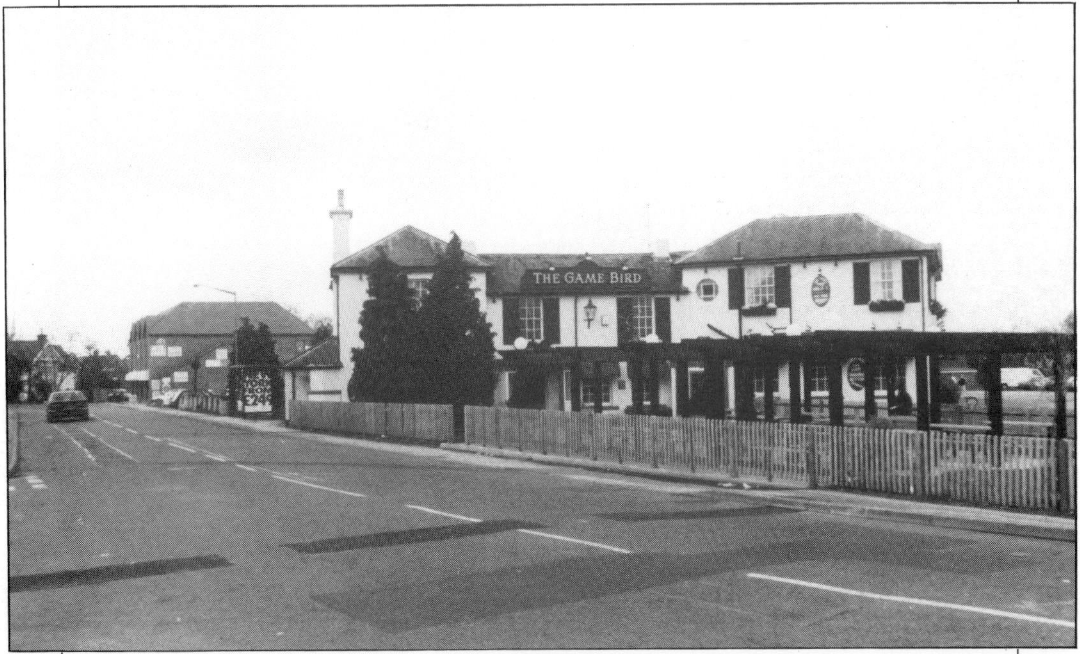

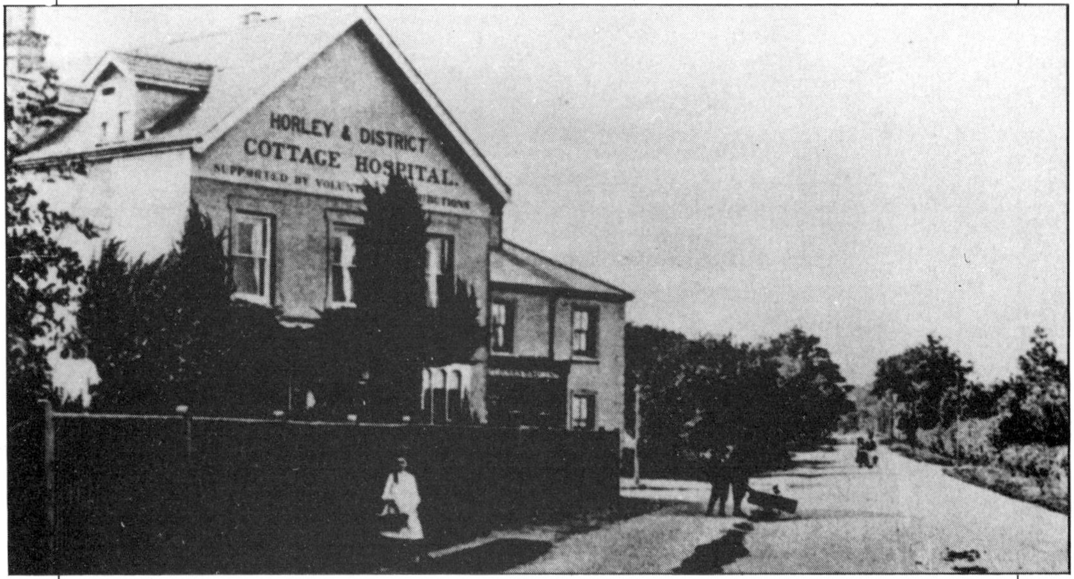

The Cottage Hospital in the days of horse and carts.

Built in 1889, Horley Cottage Hospital was originally used as a private house but was later opened as a hospital by Lily, the Duchess of Marlborough in 1903. Today it has been pulled down and replaced with flats, as the 'before' and 'after' pictures show.

In November 1986, the *Horley Mirror* received a vivid account of what life was like at the hospital in 1953. Mr L. Illman, writing from his home in The Crescent, Horley, recalled: "In February 1953, at the age of 36, I was taken into the hospital and spent eight weeks there, extremely ill and, for a while, as I later learned, it was possible for the worst to happen.

A modern block of flats stands on the hospital site.

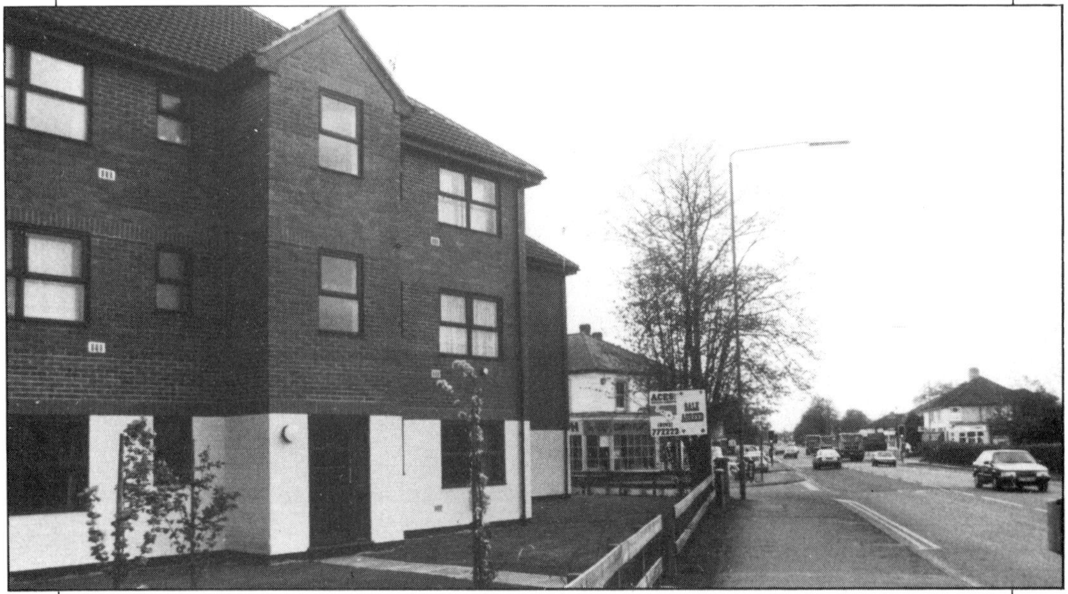

''As my room was right opposite what was then Coopers, the grocery shop, even the fact that I was still in Lumley Road, Horley, was consoling and then, as with all other nurses I have come in contact with, of those at the cottage hospital, I had nothing but the highest praise and the fact the hospital was small gave it a wonderful homely feeling. So much so, it gave the feeling of one large family living there and also, as I have lived in Horley since 1932, I knew most of the patients, both men and women.

''The individual attention that was afforded, together with the fact that I was still in the care of Dr Brown, my regular GP, I feel sure helped my recovery quite considerably. Over the years I have visited patients there, including my brother and a wartime pal of his who were taken in to spend their last days. Most of them spoke to me saying they felt comforted by the fact they were going to die in the Cottage.''

Mr Illman recalled many of the staff. There was Sister Peche, 'a very considerate lady' whose duties were that of the matron; a Welsh nurse or sister by the name of Jones; Nurse Willey, who Mr Illman used to call Dorothy Lamour, and Nurse Betty Edwards who lived at Smallfield.

''The day I was taken into hospital happened to be her 21st birthday and her party in the hospital was a 'fair do'. I think the finder in the hunt-the-parcel game may have been the nurse from Povey Cross.

''The other members of staff I remember were the cook, who I believe lived in Lumley Road; Mrs Robins; Queenie the cleaning lady and Mr Williams, who gave me many shaves. I think he lived in Charlesfield Road.''

Mr Illman's most striking memory is when a very sick young girl from Horley was brought into the next ward. ''I can still recall the sound of a woman's footsteps early every morning as she made her way to the hospital and, who, I was told, was the baby's mother. I became more concerned for her than myself. I believe her name was Covey, and that she fully recovered.''

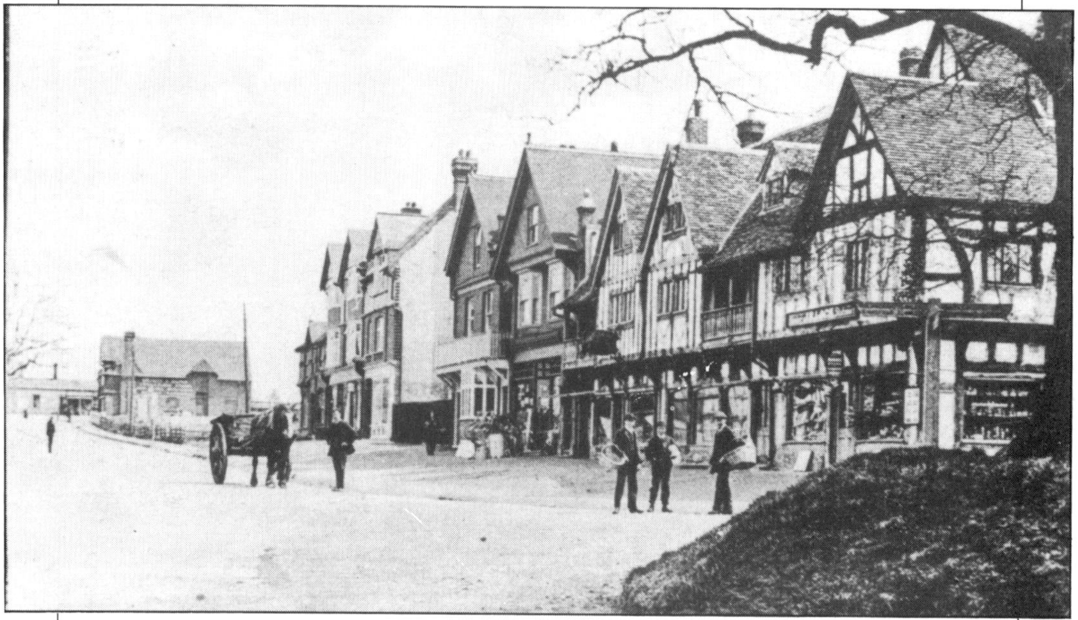

A winter's day in Station Road West, Oxted, *circa* 1908. The station can just be seen at the top of the picture. On the right, a bicycle store occupied premises later to become Oxted Linens. Today, the road is a busy shopping street containing the Post Office, The Hoskins public house and a variety of shops. A branch office of the *Surrey Mirror* operates from number 7, next door to the Plaza Cinema.

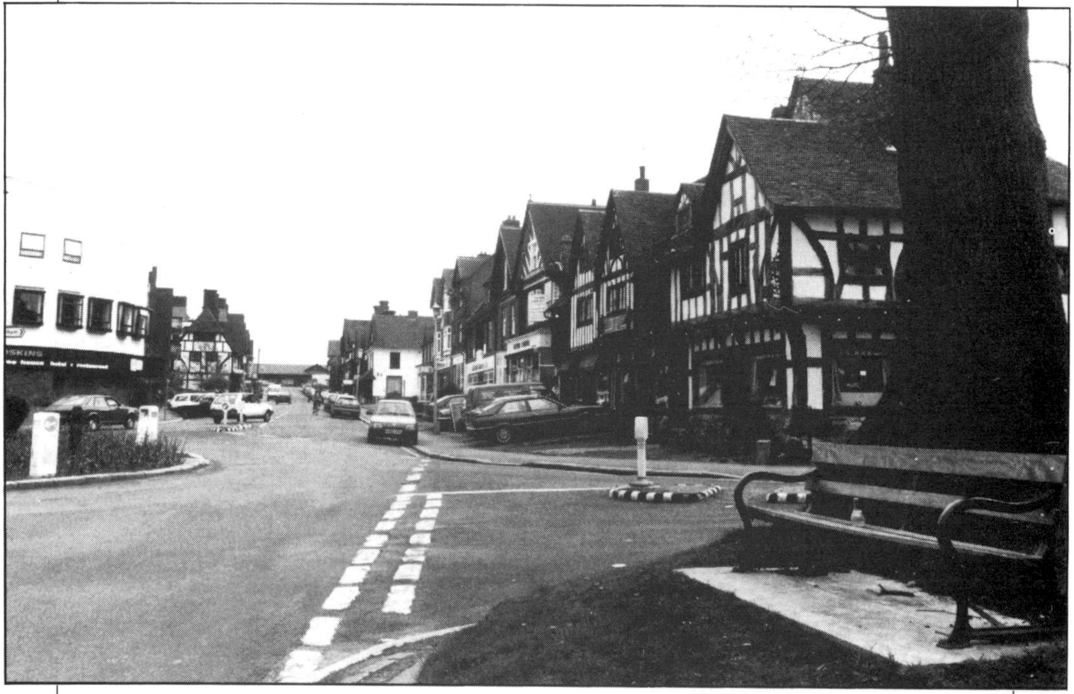

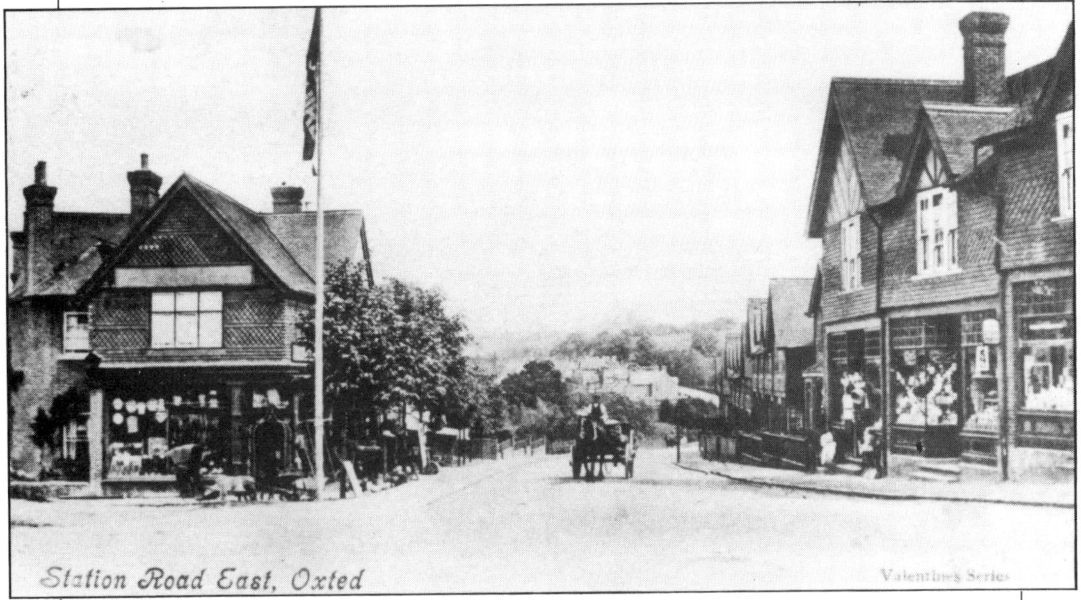

When the shops were constructed on the east side of Oxted Station, villagers called the locality 'New Oxted.'

At the bottom of the road, you can see that Snatts Hill has houses on only one side of the street, while at the top, there seems to be only a handful of shops. Standing prominently outside the ironmonger's store is a large flagpole which has long since gone. This picture has been taken from a postcard franked in 1905.

Today, this is a bustling shopping road where you can park your car only if you happen to be lucky!

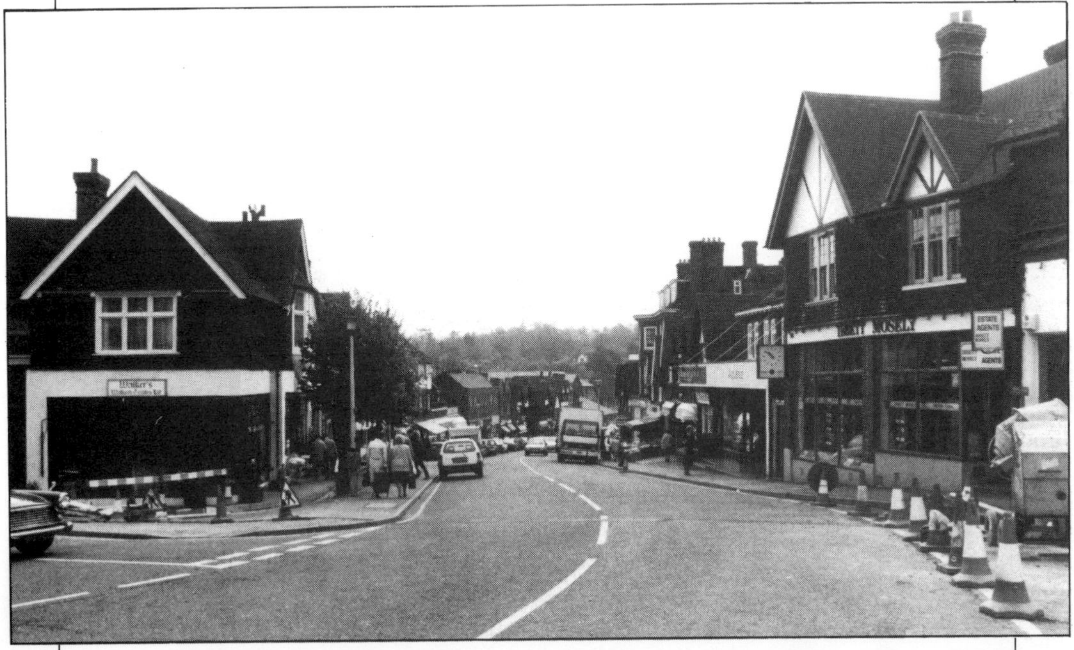

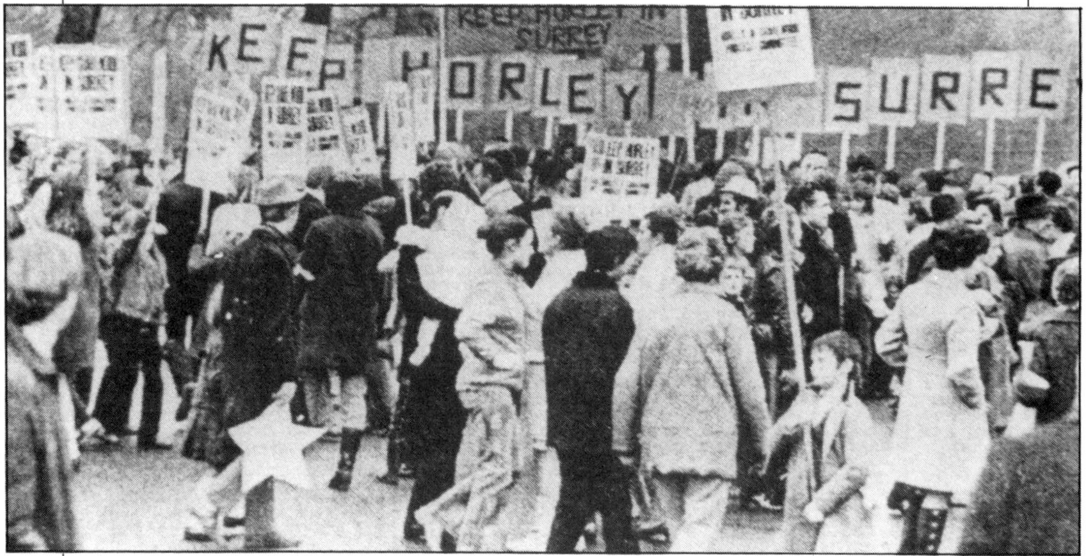

Protesters fight to keep Horley in Surrey, during a 1972 boundary battle.

Horley nestles in the southernmost tip of Surrey, bordering the administrative county of West Sussex.

When Sussex was split into two counties, following the recommendations of the Redcliffe Maud committee (1972), there was great anxiety that the town would be swallowed up by West Sussex.

Early in December 1972, the strength of feeling among anti-West Sussex protesters reached a peak with mass demonstrations in the town. The message to the government was clear: Keep Horley in Surrey.

A petition signed by 10,000 Horley residents was presented, demanding both Horley and Gatwick be kept in Surrey. On Sunday December 4, 1972, more than 2000 demonstrated against the proposal.

Placard-waving demonstrators in December 1972 block the A23 at the Cambridge Hotel, Horley.

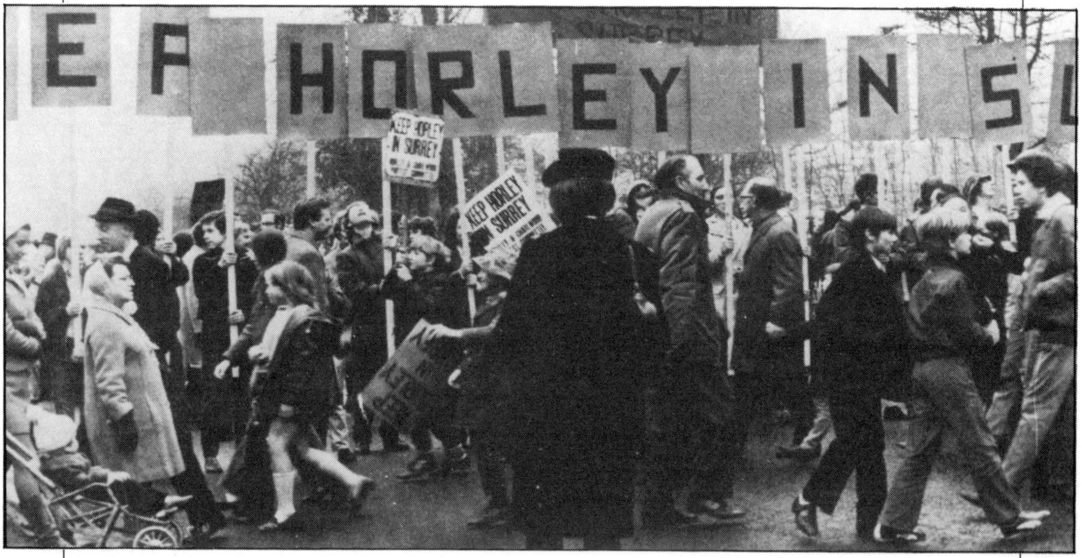

The Horley Advertiser dated Friday December 10, 1972, carried dramatic photographs of large crowds blocking the A23 London to Brighton road as they marched backwards and forwards holding up vivid placards.

"Youths in leather studded jackets, teachers and councillors, parents, children and their dogs stood side by side in the road by the Cambridge Hotel at the point where the proposed new Surrey/West Sussex borders will meet."

The main reason for the opposition was the fear that West Sussex would encourage the growth of Gatwick Airport.

The outcome was that Horley and Charlwood remained in Surrey – a decision made by the Government in November 1973.

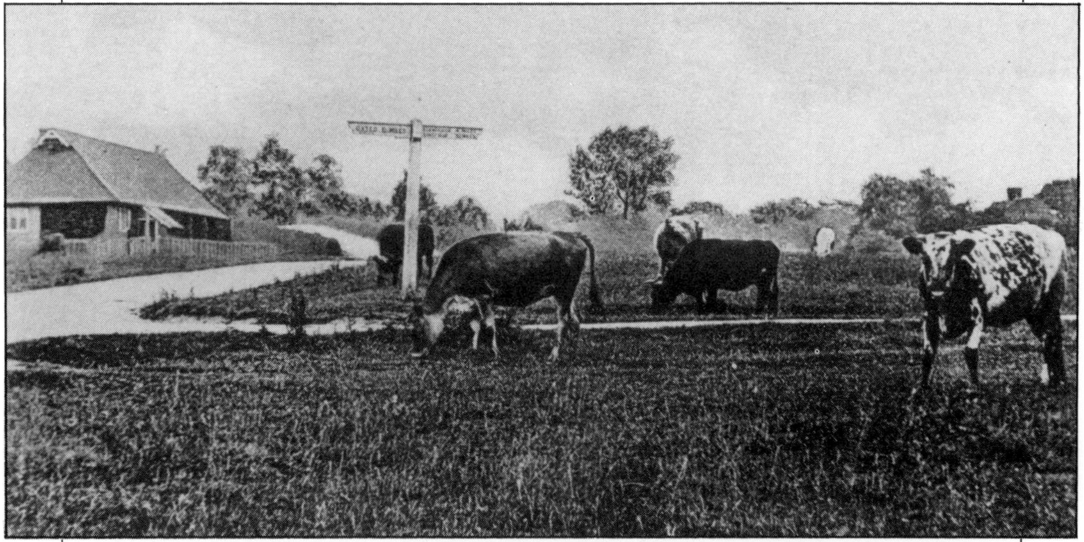

A tranquil scene in Hurst Green, Oxted, in about 1905. The old timber signpost points to Oxted 1½ miles, Edenbridge 4 miles, and to Lingfield 5¼ miles. Also pictured is the same scene in 1990.

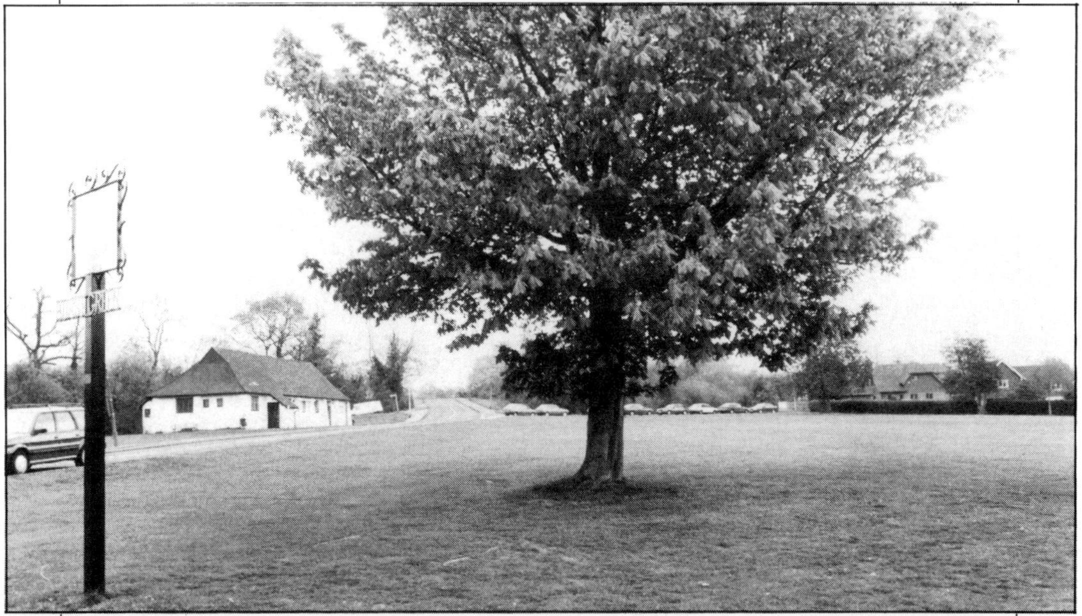

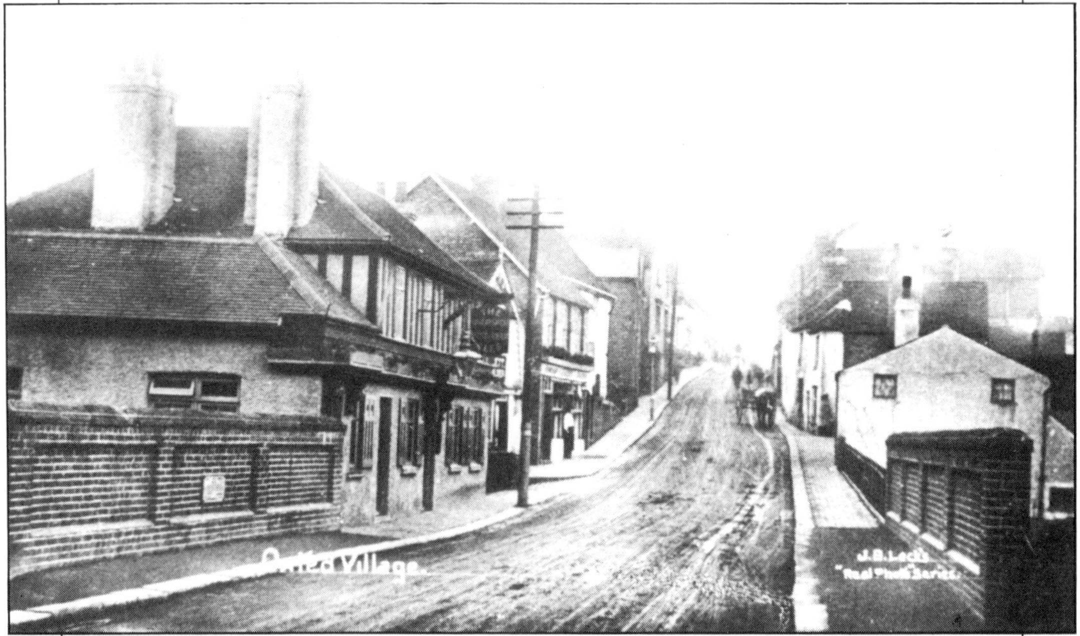

The main A25 used to go straight through Old Oxted, which today is still an 'olde worlde' narrow high street, retaining much of its charm. Obviously the sender of the postcard this picture was taken from enjoyed living in the town. He wrote on the back 'There's no place like home'.

The A25 is now diverted away from the old town, enabling a village atmosphere to thrive.

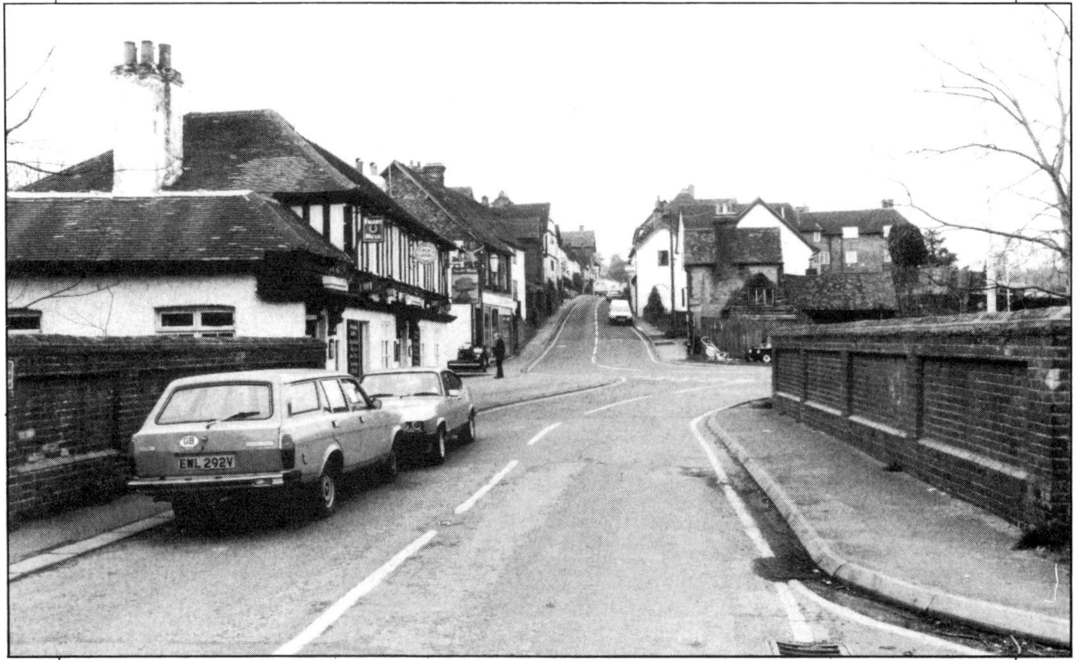

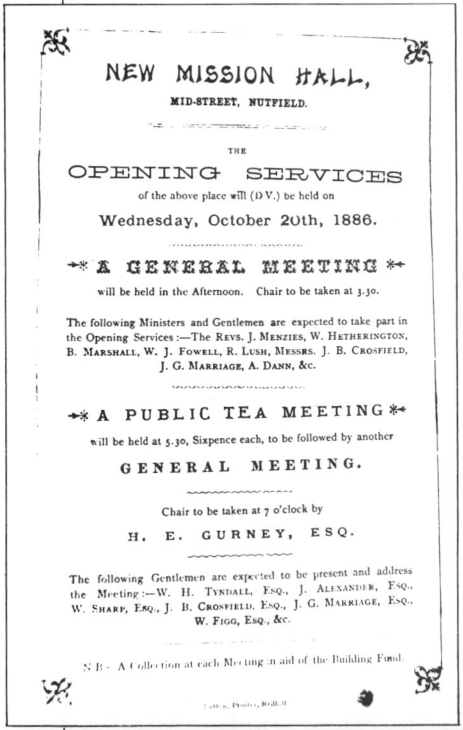
NEW MISSION HALL,
MID-STREET, NUTFIELD.

THE
OPENING SERVICES
of the above place will (D.V.) be held on
Wednesday, October 20th, 1886.

A GENERAL MEETING
will be held in the Afternoon. Chair to be taken at 3.30.

The following Ministers and Gentlemen are expected to take part in the Opening Services:—The Revs. J. Menzies, W. Hetherington, B. Marshall, W. J. Fowell, R. Lush, Messrs. J. B. Crosfield, J. G. Marriage, A. Dann, &c.

A PUBLIC TEA MEETING
will be held at 5.30, Sixpence each, to be followed by another
GENERAL MEETING.

Chair to be taken at 7 o'clock by
H. E. GURNEY, ESQ.

The following Gentlemen are expected to be present and address the Meeting:—W. H. Tyndall, Esq., J. Alexander, Esq., W. Sharp, Esq., J. B. Crosfield, Esq., J. G. Marriage, Esq., W. Figg, Esq., &c.

N.B.—A Collection at each Meeting in aid of the Building Fund.

A poster advertising the opening of a new mission hall in Mid Street, South Nutfield on October 20, 1886.

A Christmas play at Frenches Road girls' school in Redhill, back in 1930. The photo was loaned to the Surrey Mirror in 1986 by Mrs Joan Unsted who lived in Observatory Walk, Redhill.

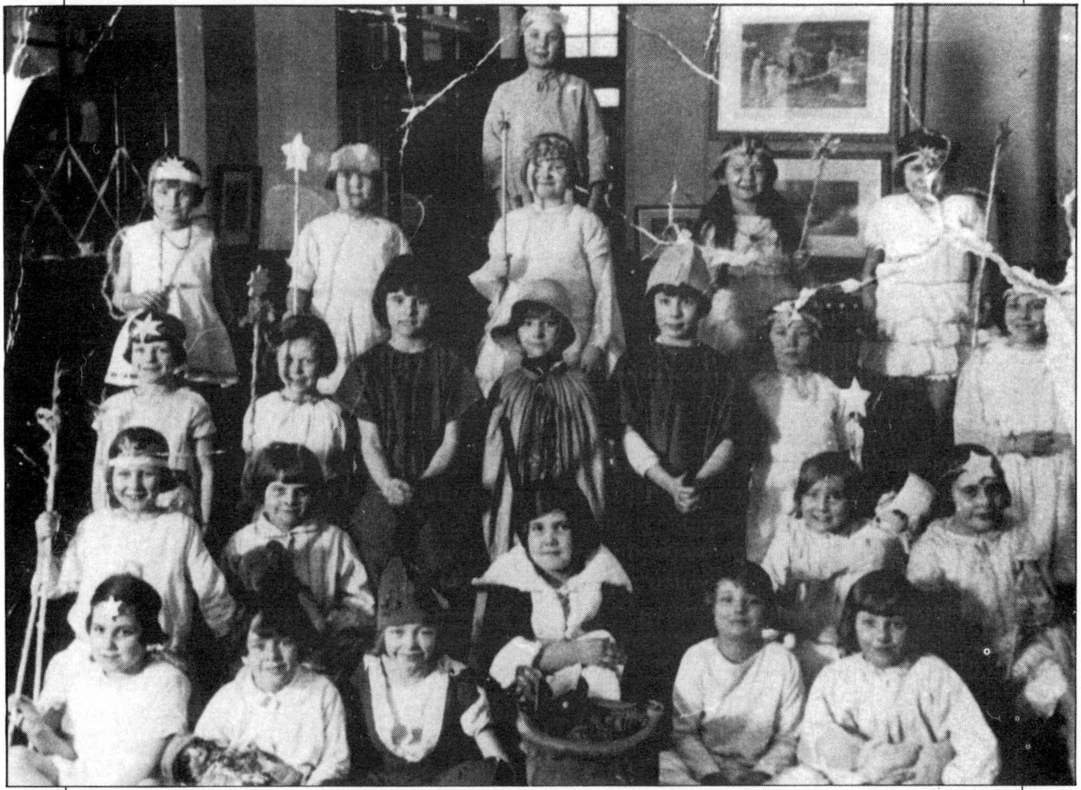

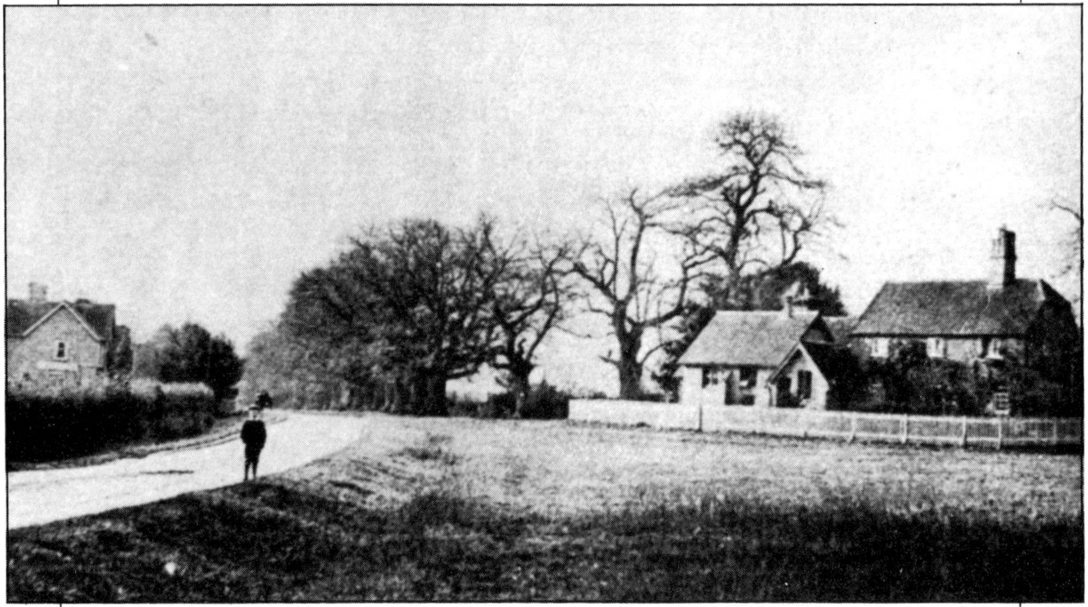

View of Felbridge in the early years of the century with the school on the right.

The mill ponds in and around Felbridge on the Surrey and Sussex border are a key to the past, for they were used in the Weald iron industry.

St John the Divine Church was built in Felbridge in 1865.

In the 1930s, a very learned medical man lived in the neighbouring village of Dormansland, at a house called The Crossways. Dr Harold Balme was born in London in 1878, and spent many years serving in China. Between 1906 and 1911 he was surgeon to Schofield Memorial Mission Hospital in Taiyuan. From 1912 to 1921 he held the position of professor of surgery at Cheeloo University, China, and became president in 1921. He wrote two books, *The Relief of Pain* and *China and Modern Medicine*.

Just north of Felbridge is Newchapel, a small community dissected by the busy A22 Eastbourne Road.

Newchapel is known for its Mormon Temple, built in 1958 which stands out prominently from the rural surroundings.

On September 5, 1958, the *East Grinstead Observer* reported on the preparations for the dedication of the temple, under the headline '1,000 American Visitors Expected At Dedication of Mormon Temple'. ''The Church of Jesus Christ of Latter Day Saints anticipate that about 1,000 visitors will travel from the United States for the dedication ceremonies of the Mormon Temple at Newchapel, which more than 65,000 people visited during the last few weeks.

''So many members of the church will be attending, that six dedication ceremonies will be held, beginning on Sunday. They will be performed by Mr David O. McKay, the President of the Church, who is flying from the headquarters in Salt Lake City, Utah.

''On Monday, President McKay will be celebrating his 85th birthday – 6,000 miles from home, but in the land of his forebears and the country where he carried out his early missionary work.''

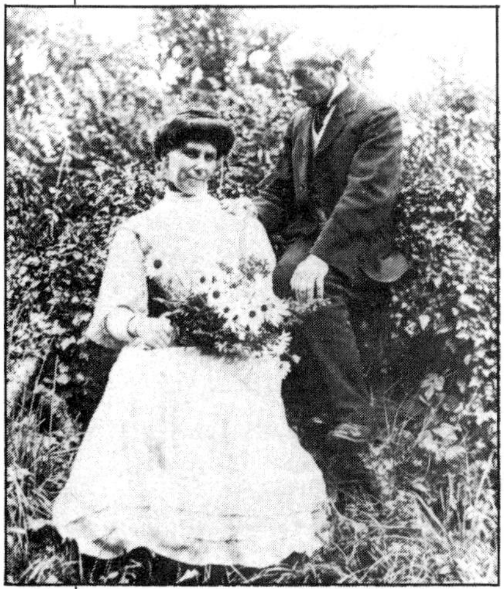

Mr and Mrs Edward Shaw who taught at Felbridge School in late Victorian times.

Mr and Mrs Edward Shaw used to run Felbridge School after their appointments in 1885. Mrs Shaw taught the infants (aged 5 to 7) in a small classroom, while Mr Shaw taught the older class (aged 8 to 14). The children wrote on slates with chalk and learnt arithmetic on an abacus.

At playtime, boys and girls were segregated on the lawn behind the schoolhouse.

A 1905 document officially names the school as the 'Godstone–Felbridge School, accommodating 75 children, 45 older and 30 infants'. In 1914, the school recorded that each child had a plot of land on which to grow vegetables.

The full story of the school is unfolded in a book entitled *The Village School – Two Hundred Years of History at Felbridge School*, published by Gordon Wilkinson with the help of Lloyds Bank.

A hot summer's day many decades ago at Felbridge School.

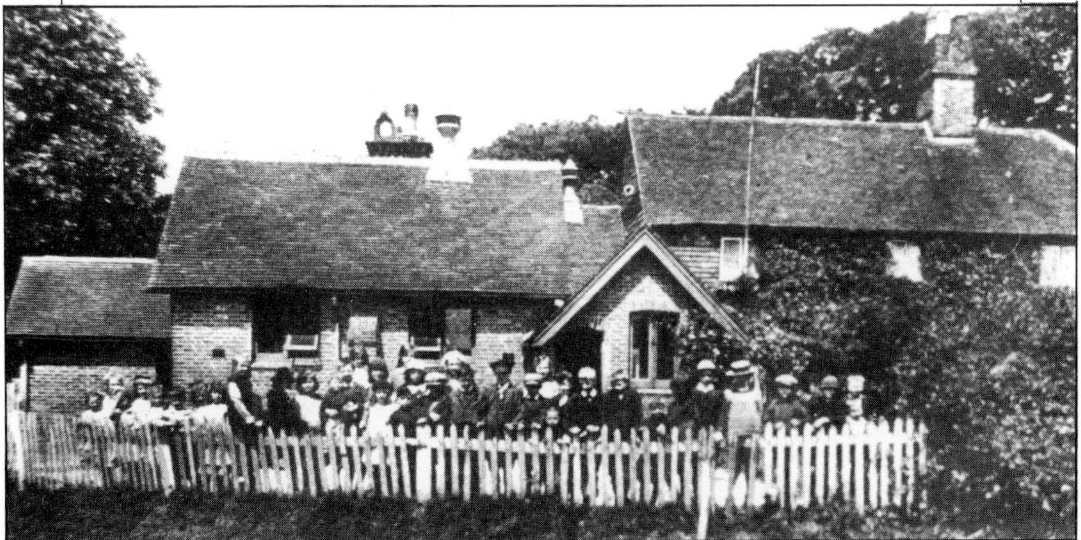

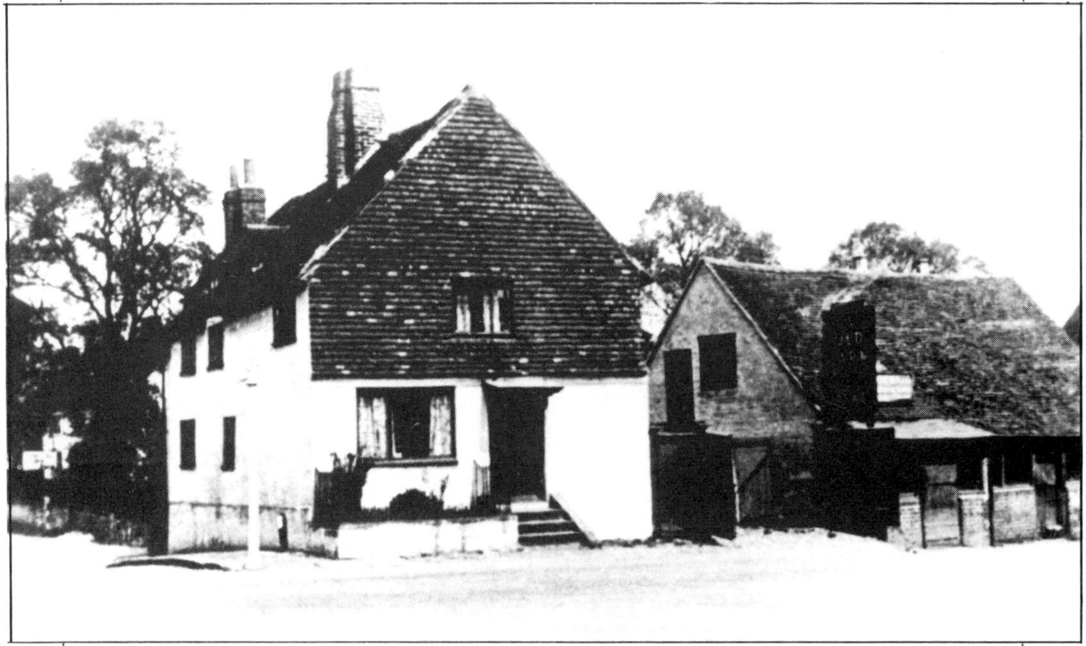

This cottage was once the home of a Miss Wren, but it was demolished as part of a road-widening scheme. The Old Farm next door sold Devonshire teas. It is now an estate agents. In the late 1980s, Miss Wren lived in Canada and reached the age of 100.

Lyle's high class mineral waters were on sale at A. J. Bird's in Bletchingley. The store also sold fruit, vegetables and fish. The Bird family were long established in Bletchingley and the widow of the little lad standing by the door still lived there at the end of the 1980s.

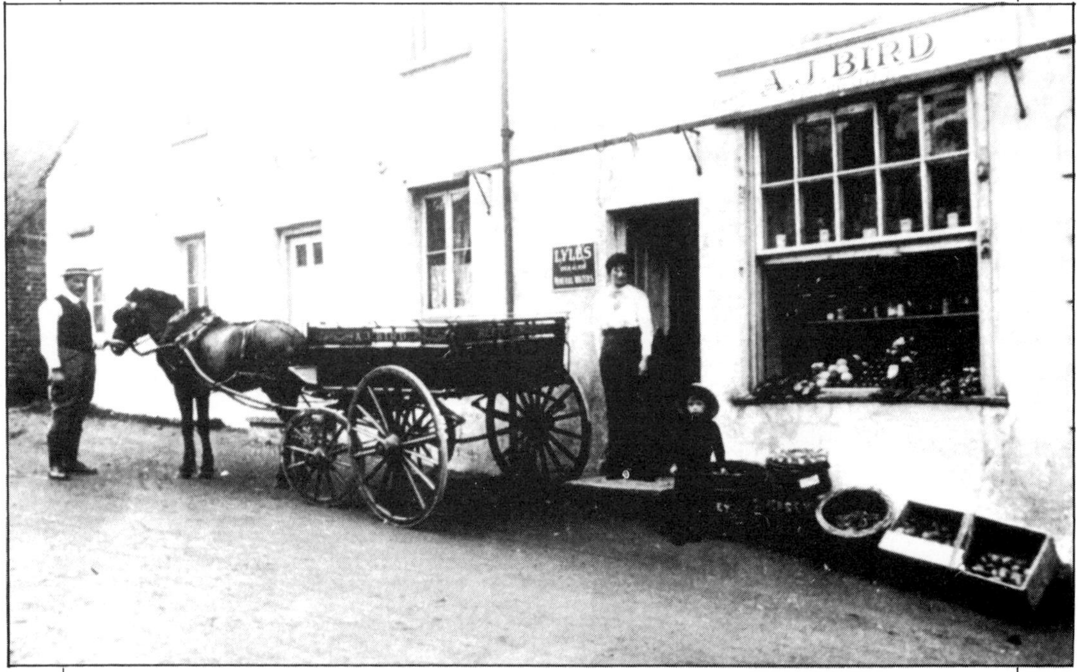

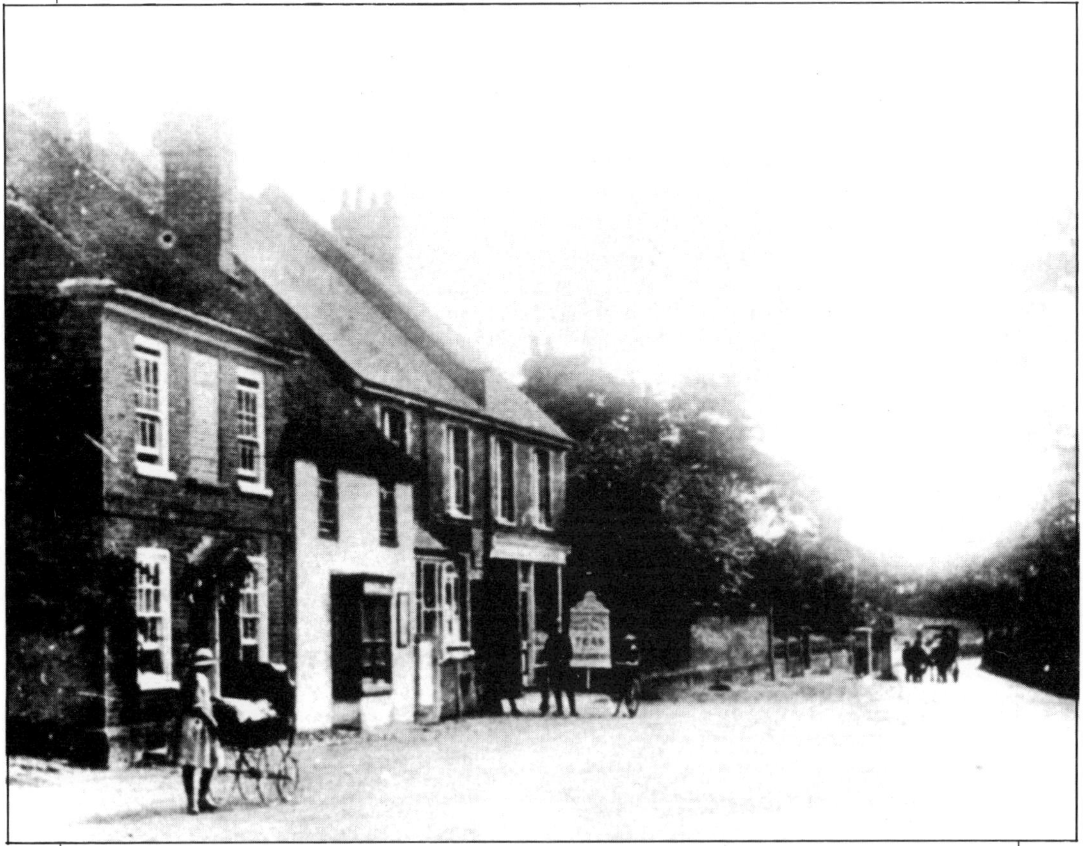

This 1924 postcard shows Outwood Road (Lane). Cyclists, prams and horse-drawn carts have since been replaced by fast cars, but at least some things never change. The Prince Albert pub still provides refreshment for villagers and people travelling along the A25. In the old picture, the furthest building was Tobbitt's dairy and the nearside of it was the post office.

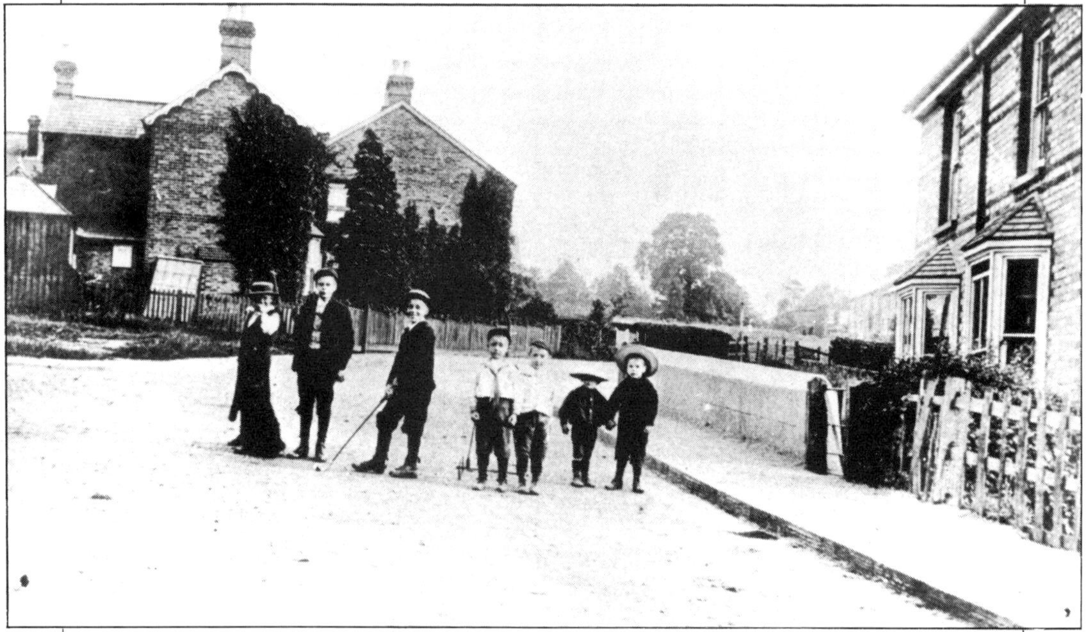

A summer's day in Barfields, Bletchingley, when playing in the street posed little danger of being knocked down by cars.

The same scene today. The children are perhaps indoors, watching videos.

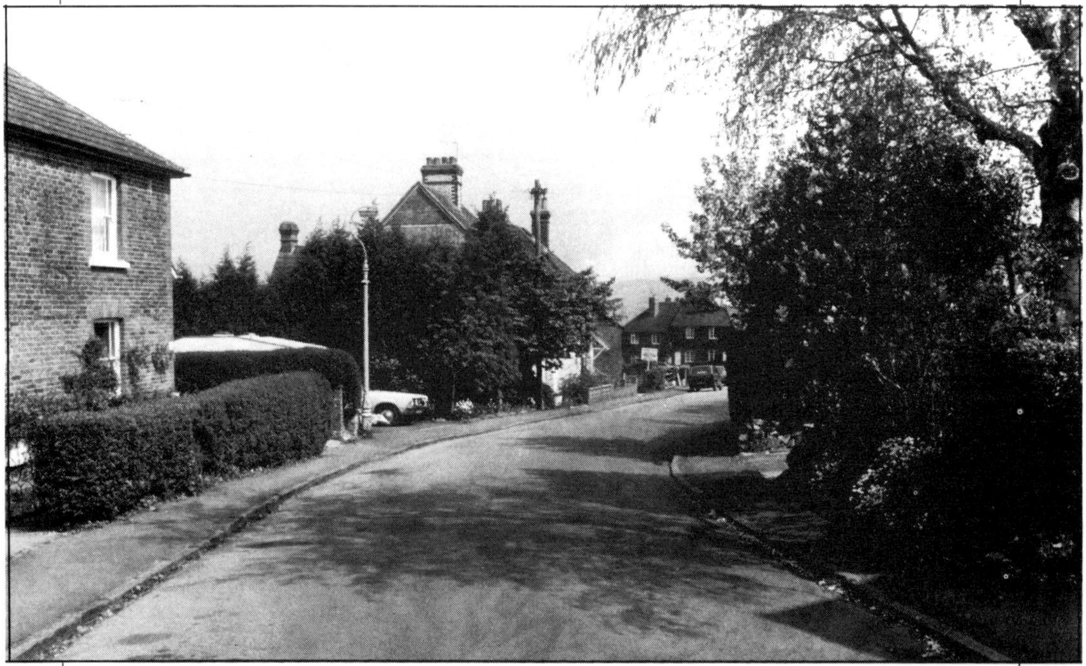

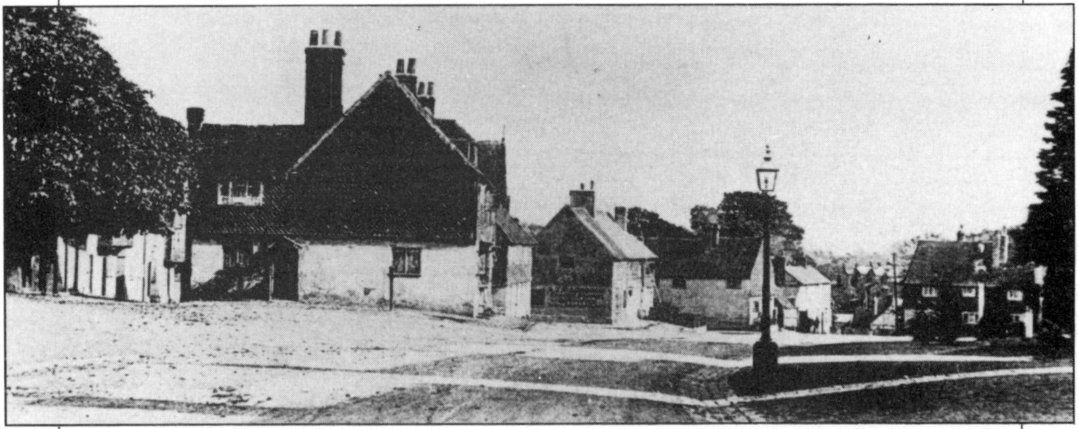

Then. . . and now. Much of the old village charm remains in the modern picture of Bletchingley High Street, despite the noise and dirt of the cars and lorries which rumble through in their thousands every day en route to either Godstone, Redhill, or the M25.

Note that the lamp-post is missing in the present-day scene. The reason for its departure was revealed recently when an exhibition of old village photographs was put on display by Mr Derek Moore. Another villager, Mr Ernie Wilson, who lived at Mill Cottage, Pendell Road, recalled how there had been a dispute over the lamp. The old gas lamp stood on the cobbles outside Glenfield House, but was a source of controversy when mains electric came to the village. The local council wanted to wire it up for electricity and said the villagers should pay. But because the light would be shed on an area wider than just the cobbled area; illuminating the road, too, the locals disagreed they should fork out. So the lamp remained unlit for several years.

In 1938 it was moved to a spot close to the driveway of the caretaker's lodge in the hospital grounds at Rabies Heath Road but, alas, its illumination was curtailed by the blackouts during the War. With the arrival of bigger ambulances, the lamp-post was in the way, so down it came again, and was rested behind a hedge. Mr Wilson, then a local builder, made an offer for the lamp in 1946, and lovingly restored it. He discovered an 1860 date embossed on the top, and to his delight

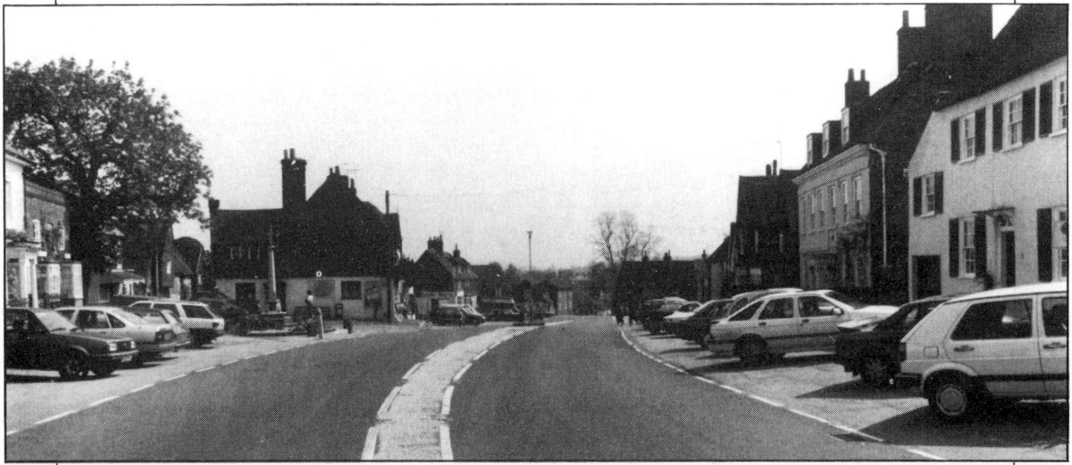

found a plaque inside giving the name William Sugg and Son Ltd, Victoria Street, London. To his amazement, Mr Wilson realised he knew the 'Son' from his days in the Air Ministry.

In the late 1980s, the lamp again shed light in Bletchingley, having been wired up at Mr Wilson's daughter's house in Rabies Heath Road.

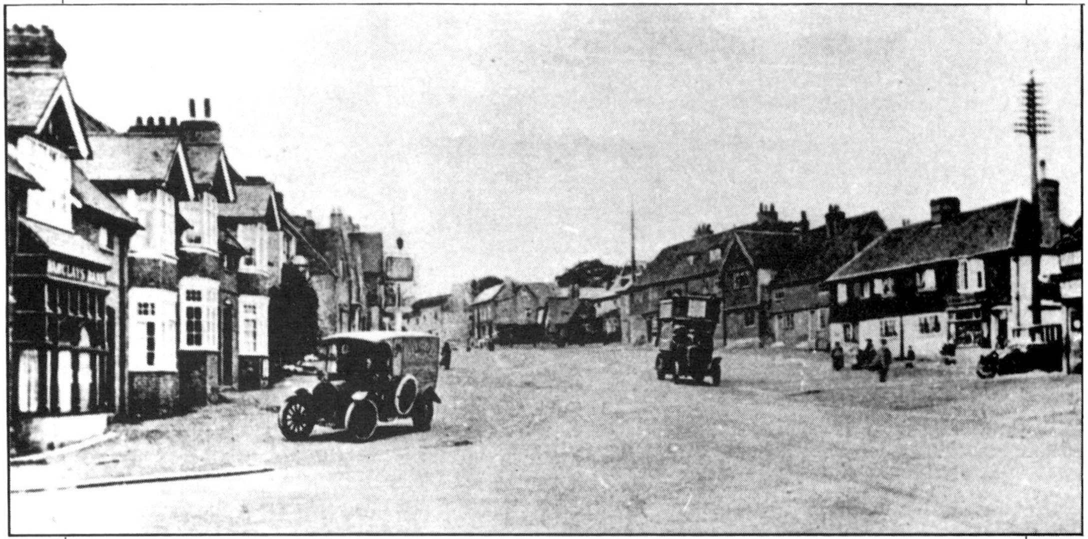

Bletchingley High Street.

Open top buses became a feature of the village as the 20th century progressed. Until recently, the London and Country 410 service between Bromley and Reigate operated along this stretch using double deckers. The service now operates only between Westerham and Reigate.

Bletchingley High Street today.

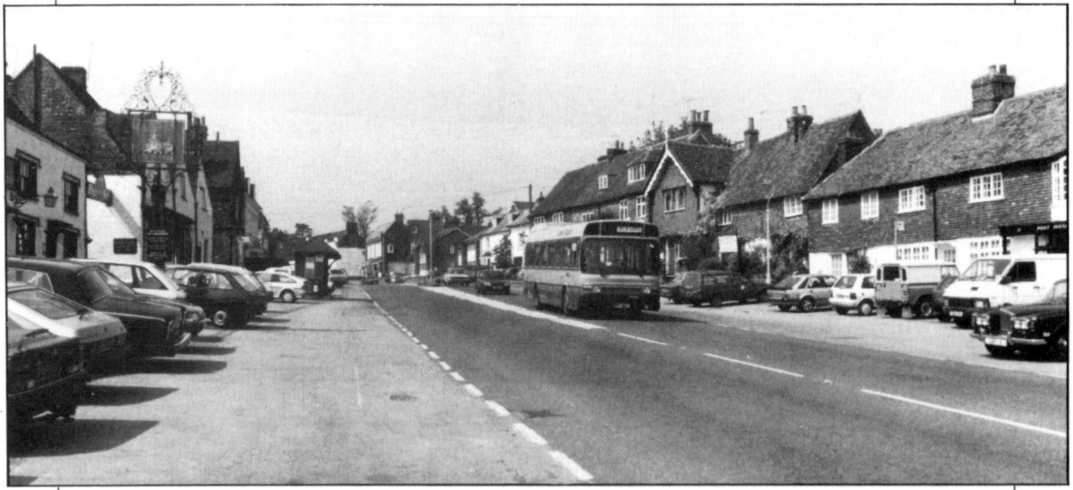

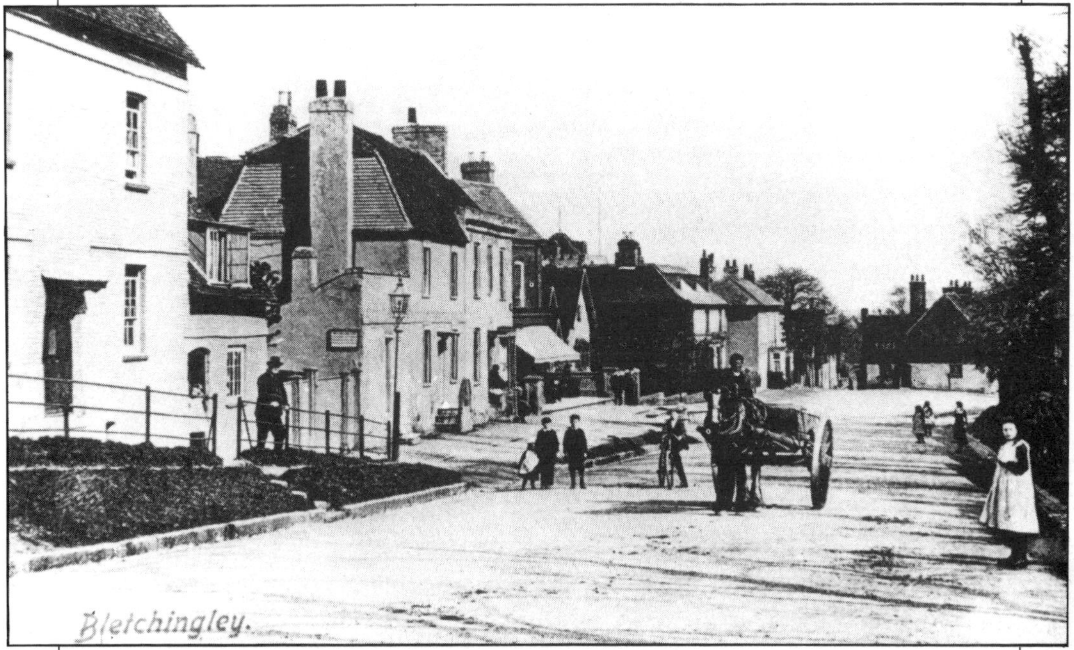

A 1905 picture of Bletchingley High Street in the days of horses and carts. Today, many of the old buildings still stand. Planning applications for development are carefully scrutinised by the Bletchingley Parish Council which meets monthly.

In the early 1800s, Bletchingley (or Blechingley as some prefer to spell it), was not just a village but a borough and market town of note, sending two members to Parliament. At the time of the Reform Bill of 1832, Lord Palmerston was one of its members. It had then about a dozen voters.

At the west end of the village stood the castle, which played a considerable part in the civil wars of the 13th century. In 1263, this castle was held for the Barons by Gilbert de Clare, Earl of Gloucester, but was captured by the Royalists.

Today, only a few slight remains of the foundations are left.

The manor was once owned by Sir Thomas Cawarden, the Master of the Court Revels, who on more than one occasion entertained his royal master, Henry VIII.

Sir Thomas gave some support to the cause of Lady Jane Grey, but Queen Mary was not able to uphold the allegations. She did, however, have Bletchingley Castle searched, and stripped of all its considerable store of armour and military accoutrements, to the value of £2000, including 16 pieces of heavy cannon.

The 15th-century manor house in Bletchingley was pulled down by Lord Peterborough, but the delightful old half-timbered gatehouse at Brewer Street survived the following centuries. Nearby is Pendell Court, a beautifully gabled Jacobean house, built by the Holmans in 1624 and now home of Hawthorns School. On the edge of the Pendell neighbourhood is the Pendell gipsy camp – an official site provided by Tandridge District Council. It rests next to the motorway between Bletchingley and the Merstham housing estate.

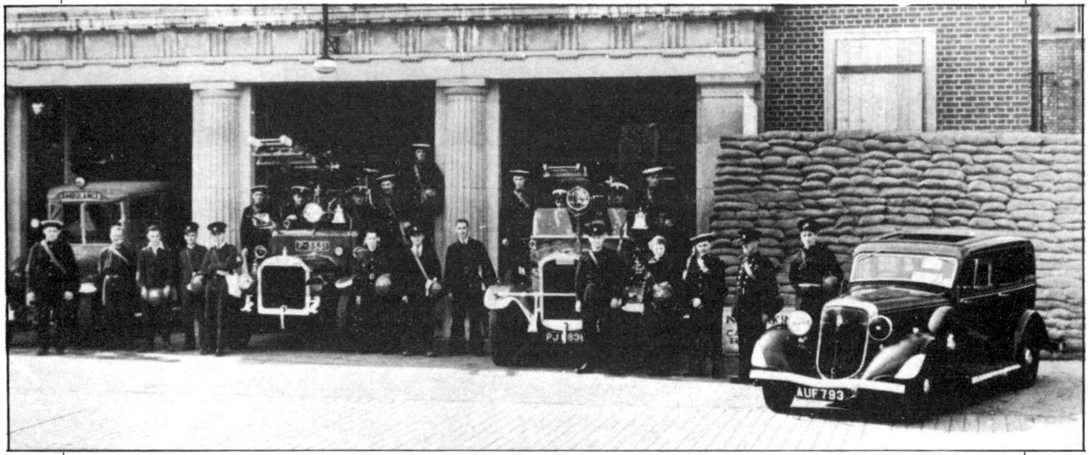

The fire and ambulance station at London Road, Redhill, during the Second World War. The building has now gone and offices stand in its place. Picture by Jack Sales.

Today, Reigate is the headquarters for the county's fire service and all 999 calls are routed through the prestigious high-tech control room next to the Wray Park Centre off Croydon Road. It is here that vigilant control room operators keep a watchful eye on incidents from all over Surrey, as they happen, and mobilise fire tenders from all the county's fire stations.

All this is a far cry from the days when horse-drawn fire carts were all that was available and by the time they arrived, your house had probably burned to the ground.

Fire fighters at Nutfield in bygone days.

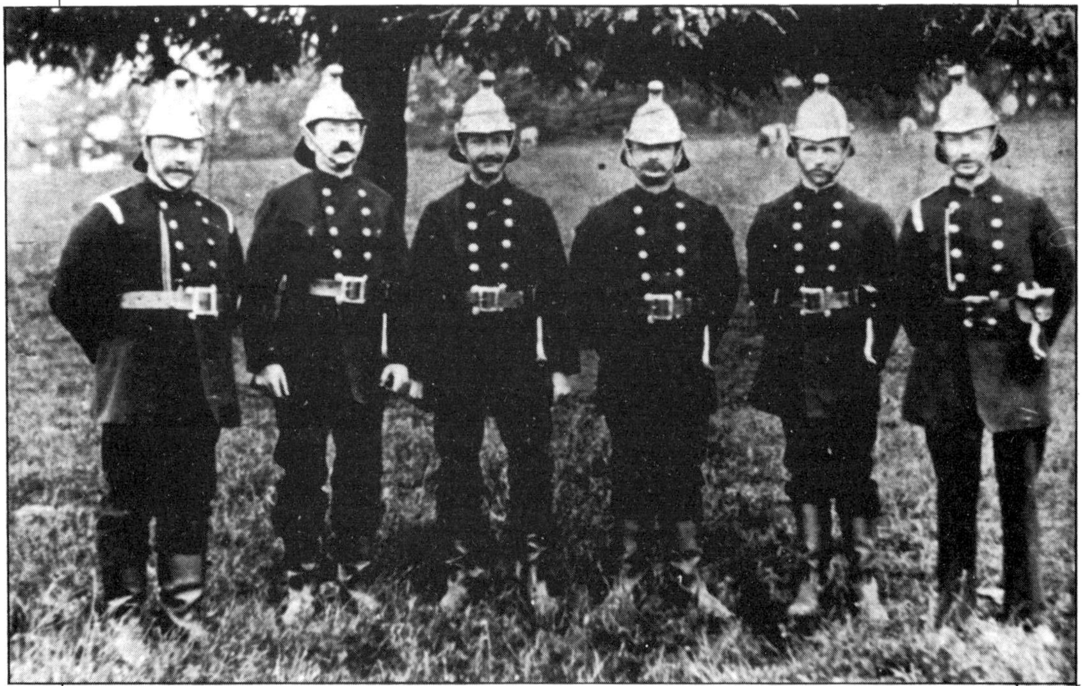

In his book of old Horley, W. H. Chouler reported how delays occurred at one such incident at Wrays Farm near Horley in June 1895. "The call came at 3.25 am, the engine left at 3.30 and arrived 'before 3.45'. The fire had been burning 'for some considerable time'. All the buildings at the farm, three miles from the fire station, were completely destroyed and eight horses, two sows and 17 young pigs lost."

In 1898, a manual fire tender was kept in a shed adjoining the Kings Head public house in Horley, and at Reigate, there are early references to two fire-fighting appliances presented by Lord Somers and Lord Hardwicke to the parish in 1809. The Vestry for the Old Reigate Borough directed the churchwardens to see that the engines were kept in good order and appointed six men to work for them whenever there was a fire. They were to receive 5s (25p) each whenever they were called into action.

Some large fires in recent years have occurred at Farleigh Court Farm near Chelsham; a warehouse at Salfords, Caterham Barracks, and several at Ryall and Edwards timber yard in Green Lane Outwood.

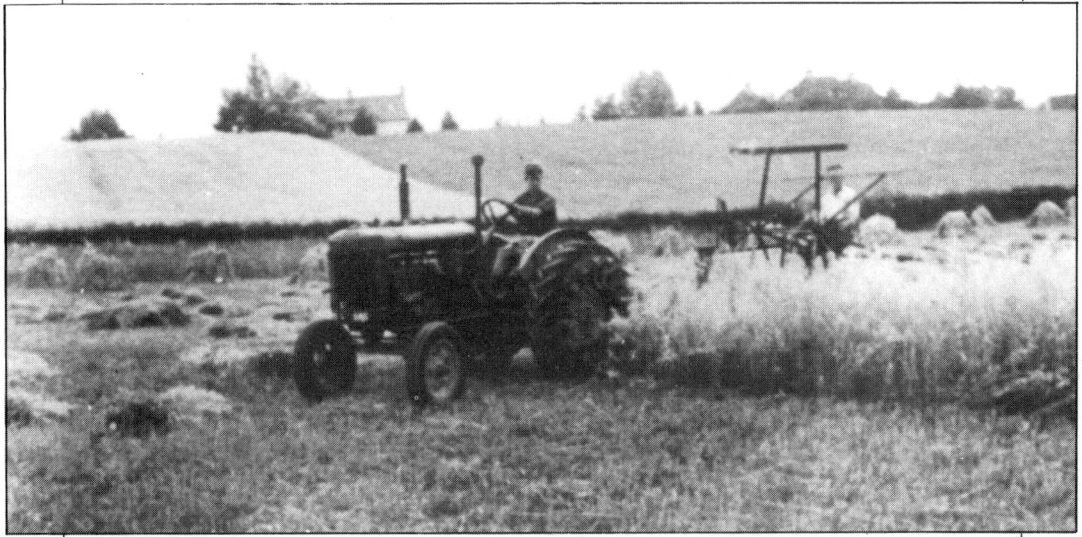

John and Wilfred Huxtable gather the hay at Trenchleys Farm back in the 1940s.

The old-fashioned way of making hay while the sun shines. In the 1940s, there was not the type of modern machinery that is available today so gang labour was used at harvest time.

With sleeves rolled up, and braces tightened, men would go out into the golden fields and 'stook the sheaves' by hand.

In the early part of the year, the gangs would arrive to help hoe out the weeds and prepare the soil for planting. During the War, Italian prisoners of war were sometimes used.

The Huxtable family farmed Trenchleys Farm, Itchingwood Common, Limpsfield Chart, in the 1940s. Mr John Huxtable and his father, Wilfred, would rise at 6.00 am to start a long day in the downland fields which would often not end until 10.30 pm.

Here is a glimpse of those farming days at Trenchleys.

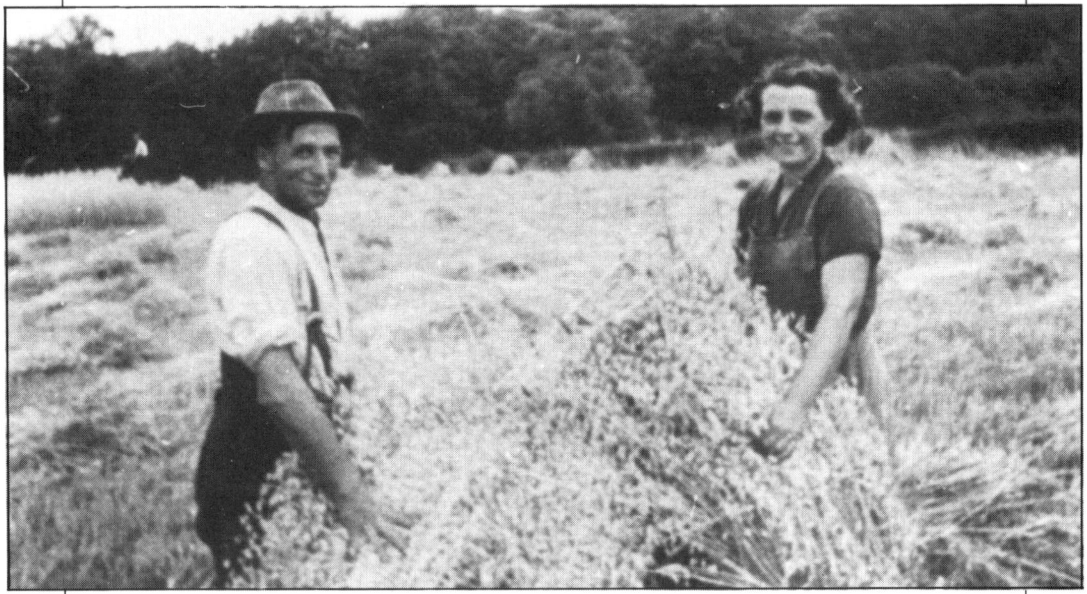

Farm helpers stook the sheaves by hand at Trenchleys Farm, Itchingwood Common, Limpsfield Chart.

Mr Wilfred Huxtable, who farmed Trenchleys at Itchingwood Common.

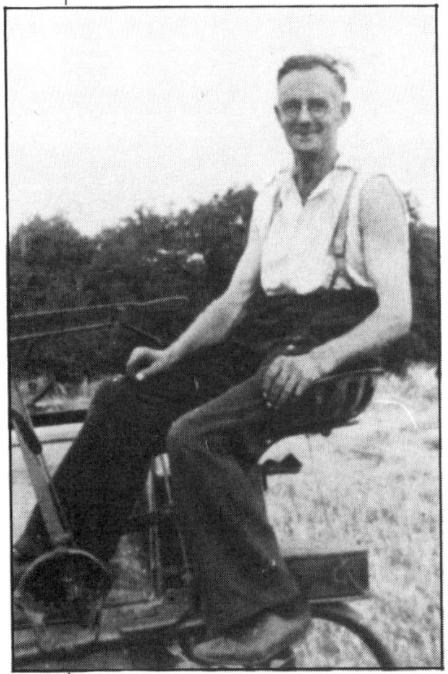

(Photos courtesy John Huxtable)

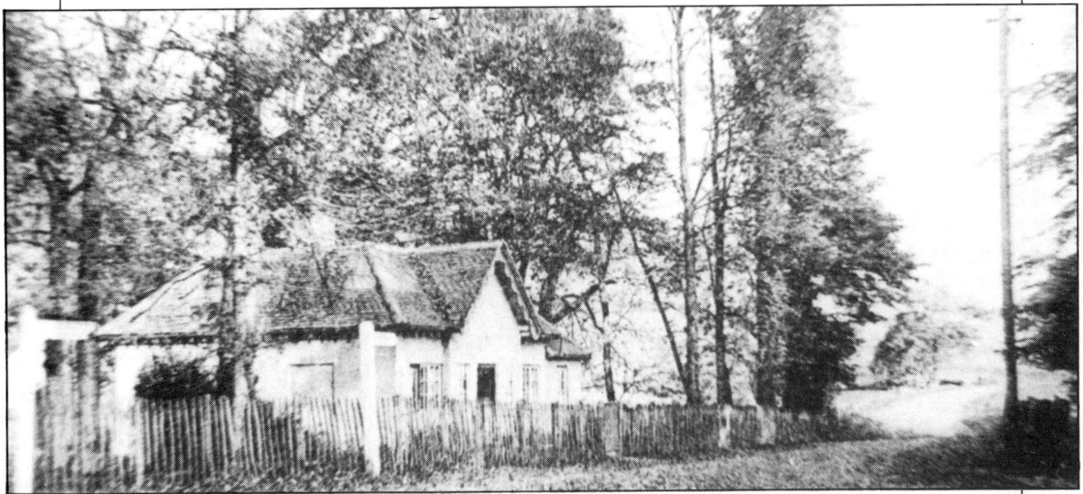

Wapses Lodge.

Succombs Hill, leading down to Wapses Lodge in Caterham, used to be a very rough road as heavy rain would gouge out channels and send stones and mud downhill in torrents.

As a dare, youngsters in the 1920s used to wheel their bikes to the top of Succombs Hill and ride down at a hair-raising speed, pedalling hard, and refusing to brake. Their battered bicycles would shoot over the Croydon Road, where the roundabout is today, and climb up Burntwood Lane on the other side, carrying their thrilled young riders. In 1987, at the age of 72, Mr George Meredith wrote: "We were honour-bound not to apply our brakes, and to pedal as fast as we could. The penalty for applying brakes at any stage was to walk one's bike right up Succombs Hill and do it all over again."

The picture shows Wapses Lodge. It was the first dwelling to be constructed in the Caterham Parish on the Croydon/Eastbourne Road, and stood near the Half Moon Inn, now a garage.

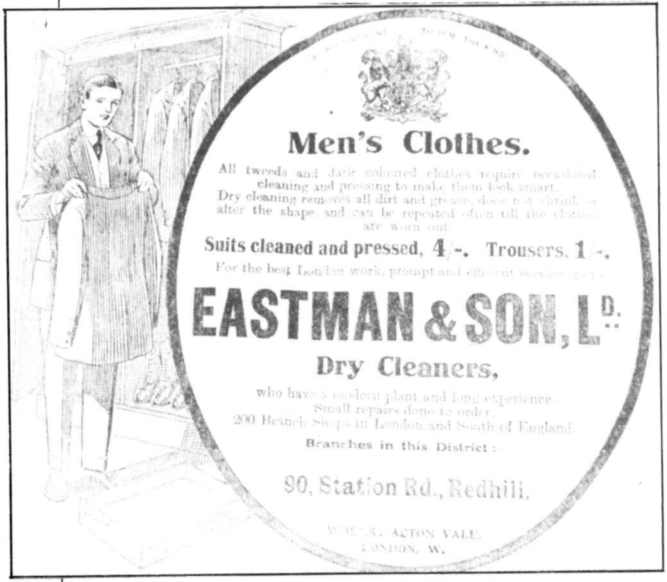

Suits were cleaned and pressed for 4/- at Eastman and Son Ltd, the dry cleaners at 90 Station Road, Redhill, in 1915, during the First World War.

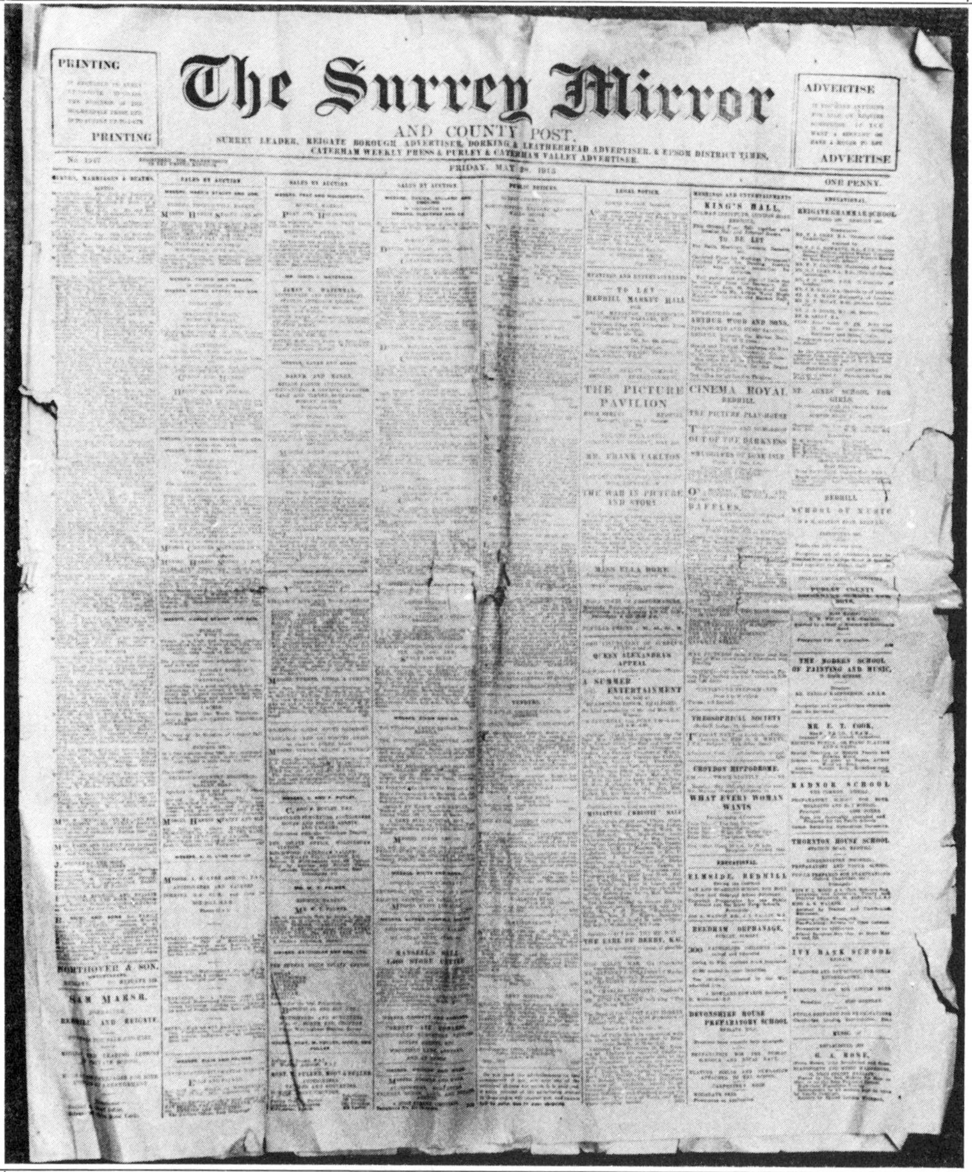

The Surrey Mirror

AND COUNTY POST.

PRINTING

PRINTING

ADVERTISE

ADVERTISE

ONE PENNY.

THE PICTURE PAVILION

CINEMA ROYAL

The Surrey Mirror and County Post of May 28, 1915. A faded copy of this edition was found in 1987 in the attic of the Brickmakers Arms in Tandridge Village near Oxted. The name 'Williams' was pencilled above the title and it is thought this referred to a resident of Crowhurst Lane End, the road opposite the pub.

The advertisements include Oxted's fortnightly cattle market and the chance to buy a 'valuable crop of mowing grass on 23 acres in South Godstone'. News items referred to moving tales of East Surrey's part in the 'war to end all wars'.

On page 7, there is news of a Caterham officer killed in battle. ''News has been received of the death of Capt. W. Hutton Williams of the 3rd East Surrey Regiment who was killed in action near Festubert on May 17. The deceased officer resided at ''Holcombe'' in Harestone Valley, Caterham and deepest sympathy is felt by the residents for the young widow and two children in their sad bereavement.''

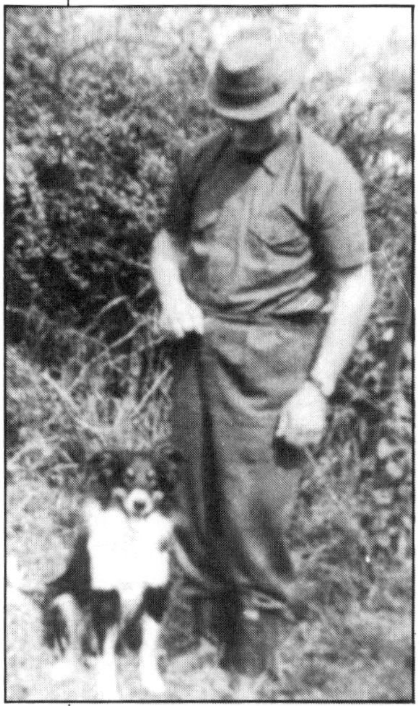

In September 1986, Limpsfield Chart mourned the death of local resident Wally Edwards whose dog, Trigger, was an expert at sniffing out golf balls while out walking on the common. While clearing out his father's garden shed, Wally's son, John, discovered three large sackfuls of balls Trigger had nudged out of the undergrowth at Limpsfield.

Wally Edwards and his dog, Trigger.

A predecessor of the London and Country 410 bus between Redhill and Bromley.

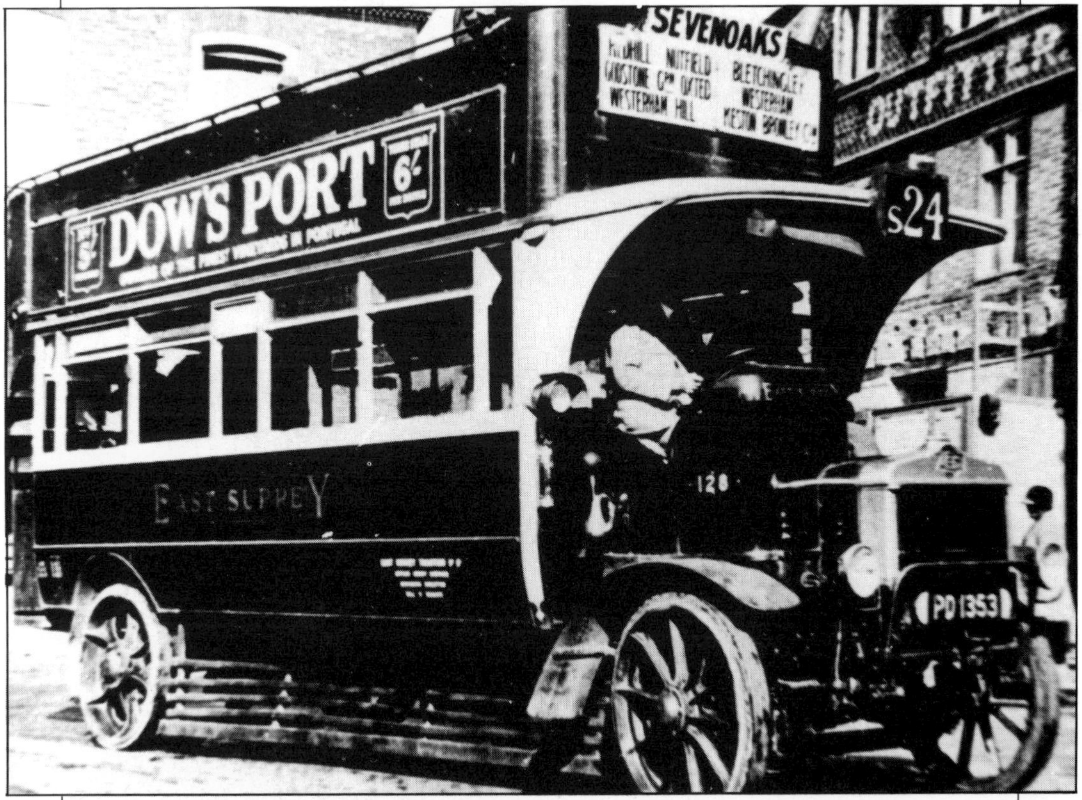

COMMUNITY THEATRES (CROYDON) LIMITED present

"MARY ROSE"

By J. M. BARRIE.

Mrs. Otery	ANNA WING
Harry	DOUGLAS RYE
Mr. Morland	RAYMOND SOMERVILLE
Mrs. Morland	BETTY BRADFORD
Rev. George Amy	HAMILTON PRICE
Mary Rose	BRENDA ROBIN
Simon	KEITH TOMS
Cameron	JORDAN LAWRENCE

The action of the play, which covers a period of over thirty years, passes between a small manor house in Sussex and an island in the Outer Hebrides.

ACT 1—The Home of the Morlands

Scene 1 ... ... As it is to-day
Scene 2 ... ... As it used to be

ACT 2—The Island

ACT 3—The Home of the Morlands

Scene 1 ... ... As it used to be
Scene 2 ... ... As it is to-day

The Play produced by HAMILTON PRICE — Setting designed by CARL BONN

Miss Robin's costumes designed by CARL BONN

Furniture by	Messrs. Blades and Messrs. Job, Oxted
Electrical and Gramophone Equipment by	John Ferguson
Managing Director	J. BAXTER SOMERVILLE
Secretary	SIDNEY W. BUDD
Treasurer	P. V. MORRIS, F.L.A.A.
Front of House Manager	...JOHN VAUGHAN
Stage Manager	PATRICK McEVOY
Assistant Stage Manager	ANNA WING
Licensees	OXTED & LIMPSFIELD BARN THEATRE CO., LTD.
Lessees	COMMUNITY THEATRES (CROYDON), LTD.

Nightly at 8.15 — Late Matinee: Saturday at 5 p.m.

REFRESHMENTS CAN BE OBTAINED IN THE ENTRANCE FOYER DURING THE INTERVALS

The Management wish to thank the Programme Sellers, who are all working voluntarily

27th March, 1939

In 1939, Croydon's Community Theatres Limited put on ''Mary Rose'' by J. M. Barrie at the Barn Theatre, Oxted, which opened in 1923.

The theatre has changed a lot over the years. The beautiful building in Bluehouse Lane appears to be much older than it is because its structural timbers came from the centuries-old saw mill barn a short walk away in Limpsfield.

In May 1923, the *Surrey Mirror* outlined the project, initiated by the Oxted and Limpsfield Players. They needed a venue but there was also a need for a communal hall to cater for varied social activities required by the growing population in Oxted and Limpsfield.

Some early artists later achieved fame, including local playwright Christopher Fry. In 1924, the July Players visited and among them were Tyrone Guthrie and Flora Robson.

NO PART OF THIS ISSUE HAS BEEN UNDERWRITTEN.

A Copy of this Prospectus has been filed with the Registrar of Joint Stock Companies.

OXTED & LIMPSFIELD BARN THEATRE COMPANY LIMITED.

Incorporated under the Companies Acts, 1908 to 1917.

Share Capital - - £4,000,

— DIVIDED INTO —

4,000 ORDINARY SHARES OF £1 EACH.

ISSUE OF 4,000 SHARES OF £1 EACH AT PAR.

PAYABLE AS FOLLOWS :—

5/- per Share on Application.

5/- per Share on Allotment.

5/- per Share three months after Allotment and the balance of 5/- per Share six months after Allotment.

Shareholders desirous of paying up their Shares in full on Allotment may do so, but no interest will be payable on the amounts paid in advance.

The Minimum Subscription upon which the Directors will go to allotment is 2,500 Shares.

Directors:

SIR ERNEST JOHN PICKSTONE BENN, Blunt House, Oxted, Surrey, Baronet, C.B.E. (*Chairman*).

ALFRED WILLOUGHBY ATKYNS, Sapperton, Limpsfield, Surrey, Esquire.

LEWIS GEORGE FRY, Stonycroft, Limpsfield, Esquire.

GRANVILLE CHARLES GRESHAM LEVESON GOWER, Titsey Place, Limpsfield. Esquire, J.P.

CHARLES HOSKINS MASTER, Barrow Green Court, Oxted, Esquire, D.L., J.P.

THE REVEREND GERALD GURNEY RICHARDS, M.A., The Rectory, Limpsfield, Clerk in Holy Orders.

BERNARD CRADOCK ROBINSON, Burghfield, Oxted, Esquire.

HARRY GORDON WHITMORE, Pilgrims Hatch, Oxted, Esquire.

Bankers:

LLOYDS BANK LIMITED, Oxted Branch.

Solicitor:

Mr. J. F. W. WHEELER, Station Road West, Oxted.

Auditor:

Mr. F. C. ALLWORK, F.C.A., (Messrs. Duncan Allwork & Co.) 39 Coleman Street London, E.C.

Architects:

Messrs. MATHEWS & RIDLEY, East Grinstead, Sussex.

Secretary (*pro. tem.*):

Mr. J. H. CLIFFORD BRILL, Sydney House, St. James' Road, East Grinstead, Sussex.

Registered Office:

The Office of the Solicitor to the Company, Station Road West, Oxted.

The original prospectus for shares in the Oxted and Limpsfield Barn Theatre Company Limited. A total of 4,000 shares were issued at £1 each. Chairman of the company was Sir Ernest John Pickstone Benn, of Blunt House, Oxted. Another familiar name on the board was that of Mr Charles Hoskins, Master of Barrow Green Court, Oxted.

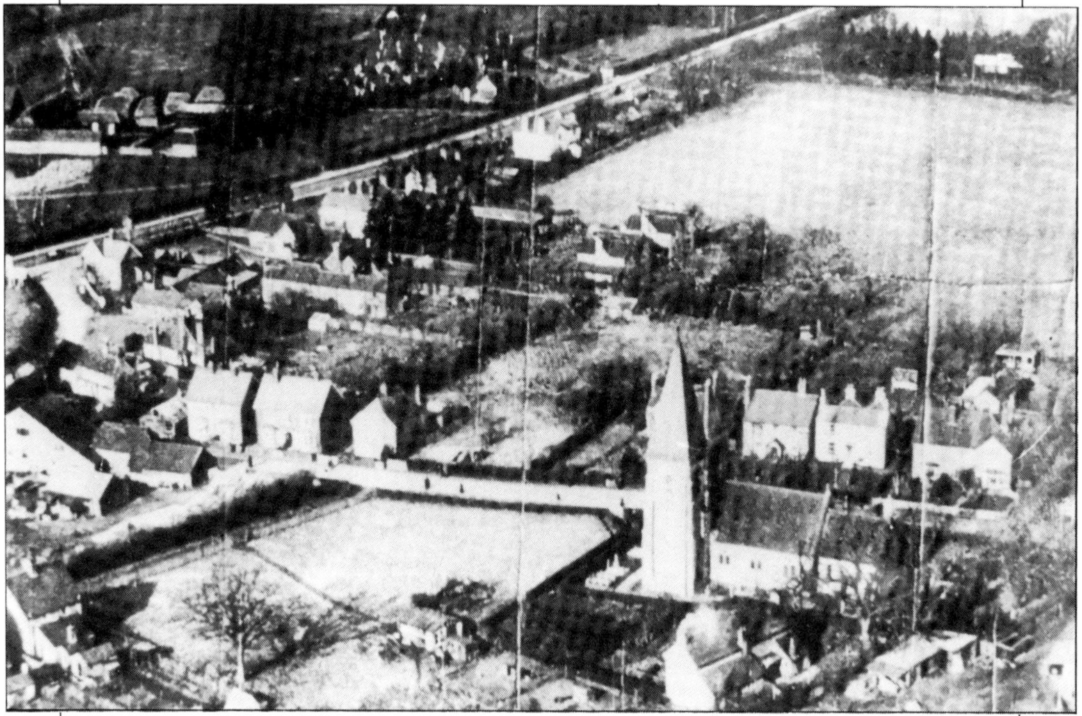

Lowfield Heath in the late 1950s.

Lowfield Heath Garage.

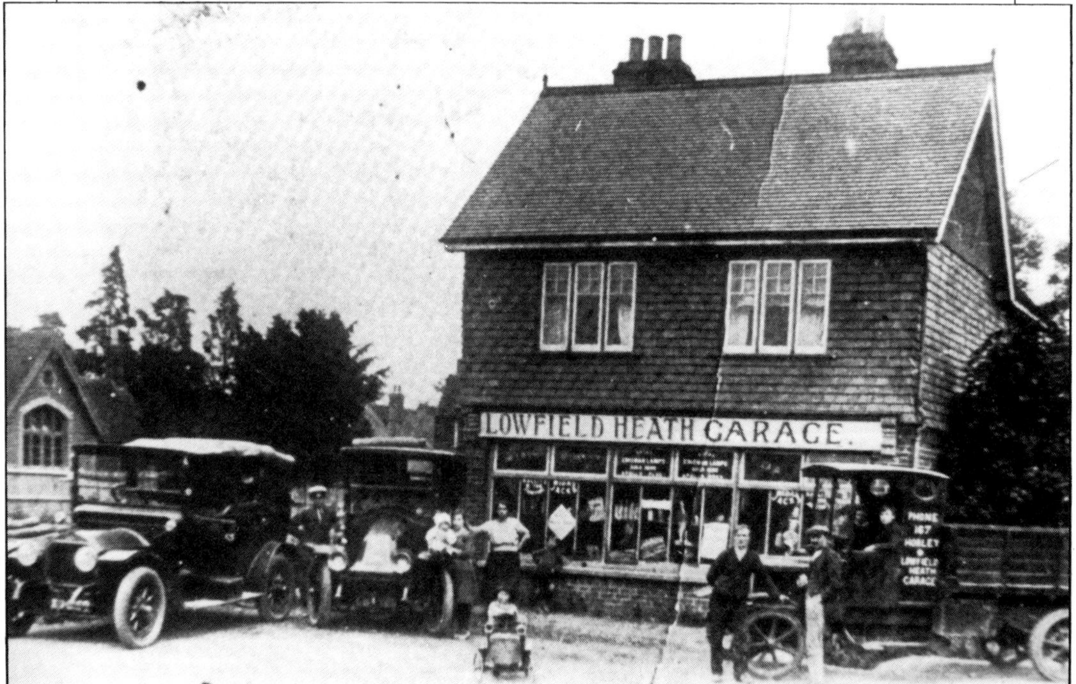

Much of the old village of Lowfield Heath near Horley has been swallowed up by the expansion of Gatwick Airport in the last three decades. The pictures on pages 32 and 34 capture those bygone days long before the airport really took off in the late 1950s.

In 1986, Mr Ernest Pett from Concord, Canada, wrote his recollections of the village in *The Horley Advertiser*, now *The Horley Mirror*. He moved to Lowfield Heath in October 1928 from Cheam and his younger daughter was born there in 1929. The family lived at Rowley Cottage, part of Rowley Farm, and within a few days of moving in, the milkman delivered some friendly advice. He suggested that the Petts should keep chickens.

Mr Pett recalled: "My wife bit the bait and bought six black Leghorns from him. They were placed in the cow barn overnight and in the morning, had disappeared into a copse never to be seen again – we owned them less than 24 hours."

The experience did not put them off keeping hens. Later they acquired more than 200 chickens – the majority of them raised from chicks bought at the McKechnie poultry farm on Charlwood Road.

Mr Pett recalled many of the village characters, such as a Mr Miller, the smithy, who also swept chimneys, and a Mr Plumridge who operated the petrol and service station located on the Brighton Road close to Horley.

The Petts were very involved with the scout troop and life at St Michael's Church. Mrs Pett was captain of a Horley Guide Company and treasurer of the Lowfield Heath WI under the presidency of Mrs McKechnie. Soon after 1930, the Petts remember looking after Reverend Hopkins while the rectory was being redecorated over several months. When the work was finished, the rector was reluctant to leave the family and tried to prolong his stay.

The rector's predecessor was remembered by Mrs Pett for his disapproving looks whenever he peered into her pram and saw her two baby daughters inside. "He used to tut-tut, and say: 'Very close together aren't they?' " recalled Mrs Pett.

The Pett family left England in 1947 and set up home in Montreal, but say they will always have fond memories of the vanished village of Lowfield Heath.

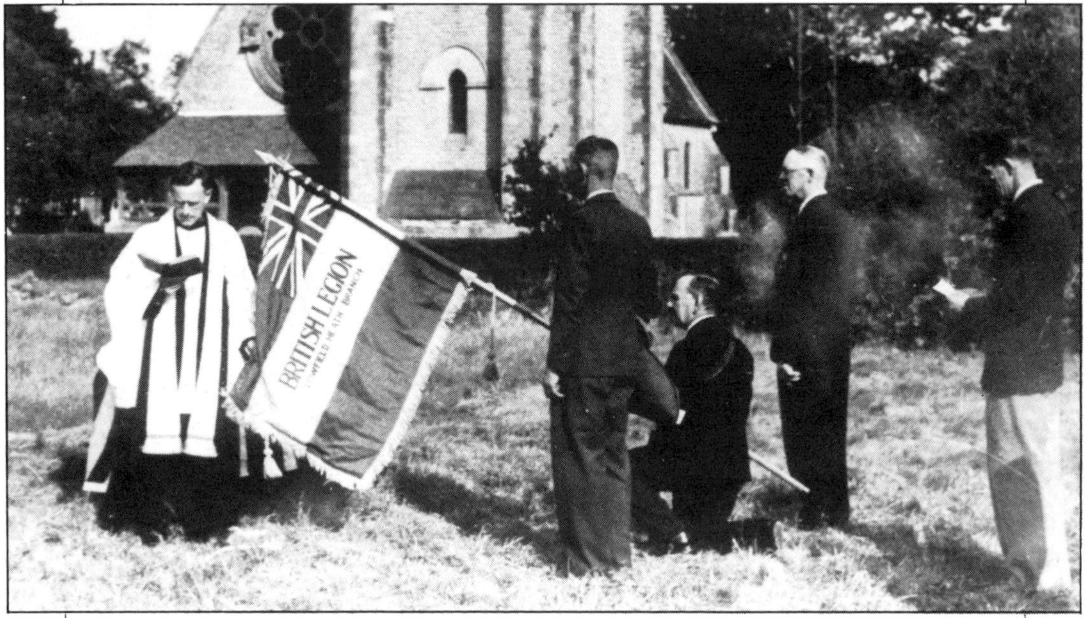

The Lowfield Heath branch of the British Legion was formed in 1947 and these photographs were taken soon after, in Lowfield Heath, just south of Horley.

Mr Bob Atkins, who led the parade, on the left of the picture, was a founder member of the branch. The officiating minister was Reverend Shergold. Mr Atkins served in the Royal Navy as a telegraphist during the two world wars. He was mentioned in dispatches and decorated for his services in the convoys to Russia. For many years he was the official standard bearer for the branch and, on one occasion, had the honour of carrying the British Standard at a Festival of Remembrance in the Albert Hall. He died in 1973.

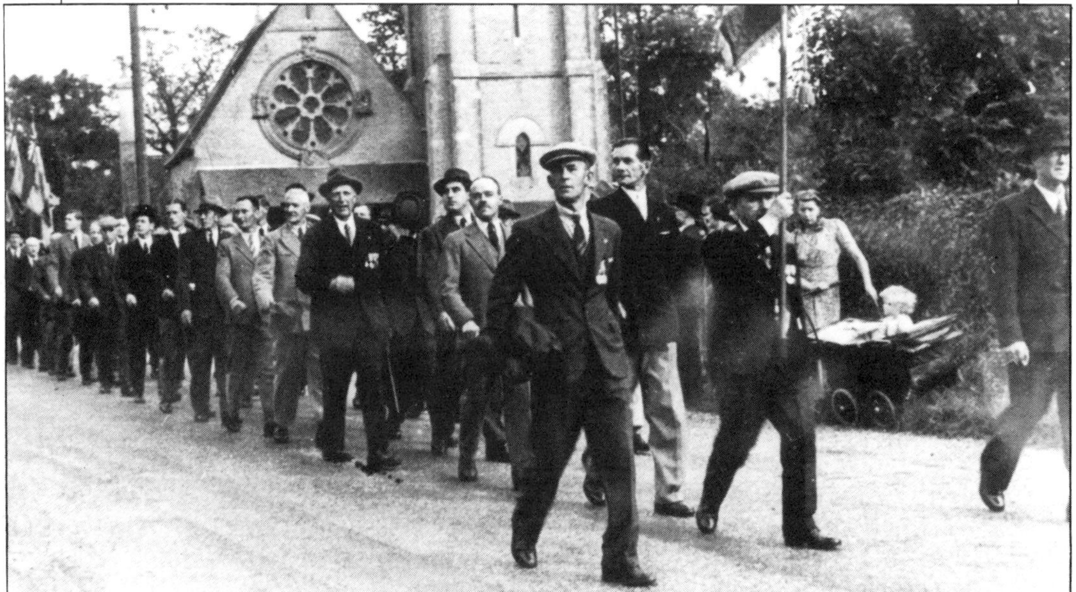

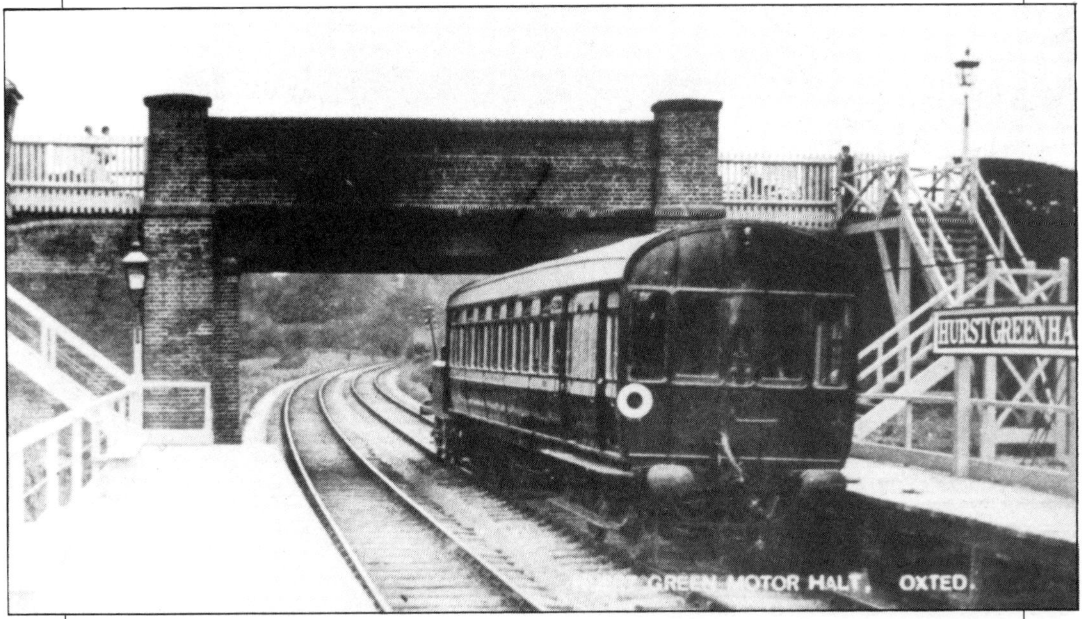

Hurst Green Halt was opened in 1907 during the month of June. The bridge to the south of the station was later rebuilt and the wooden stairs and old gas lamp replaced. Nearby Oxted Station was opened in 1884.

Below, a steam train passes over the A25 at Oxted in about 1952. These pictures, and many more tracing the history of the rural lines through the Tandridge district can be found in the book, *Branch Lines to Tunbridge Wells from Oxted, Lewes and Polegate*, compiled by Vic Mitchell and Keith Smith and published by Middleton Press.

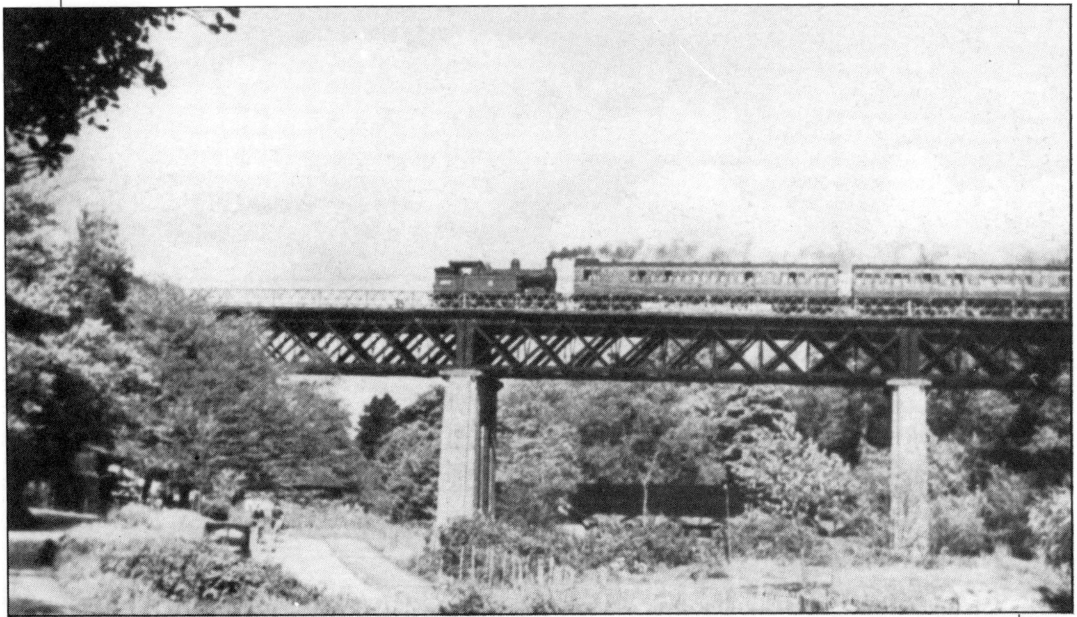

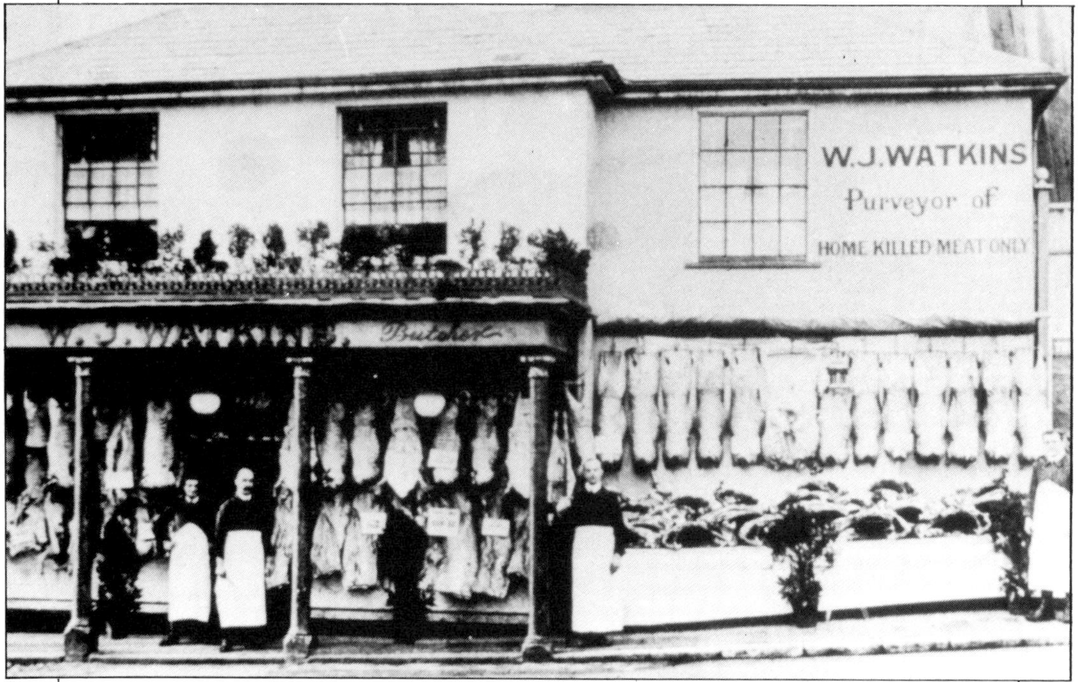

Carcasses hang outside W. J. Watkins, the butcher's in this yesteryear scene from Park Lane, Reigate. The premises still sell quality meat to townsfolk and the design of the shop retains much of its 'olde worlde' charm.

The Jersey Dairies of Redhill provided the daily 'pinta' in the town.

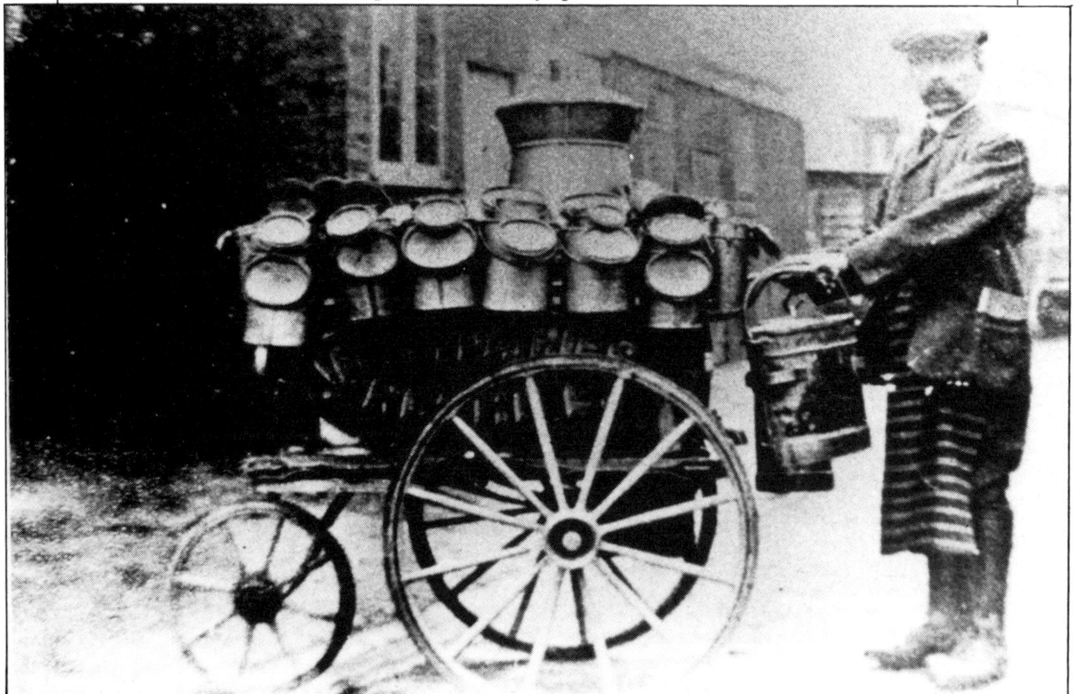

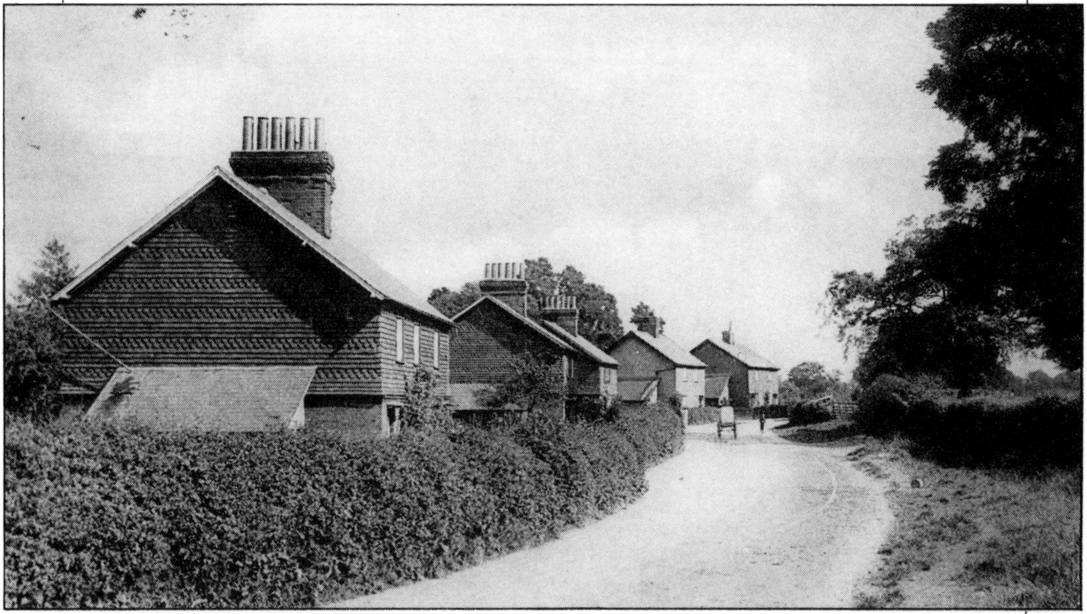

Not much has changed in Old School Lane, Brockham over the past 70 years – except the modes of transport.

In several comparison pictures in this book, the loss of trees can be noted. Some have come down to make way for development, others have died of 'natural causes'. More recently, two major storms have claimed up to two million trees in Surrey. The worst, on October 16, 1987, wiped out large areas of woodland. Scenes of the devastation are recorded in the book *Surrey In The Hurricane*. On January 25, 1990, several hundred thousand trees were felled by winds exceeding 90 mph which tore across East Surrey.

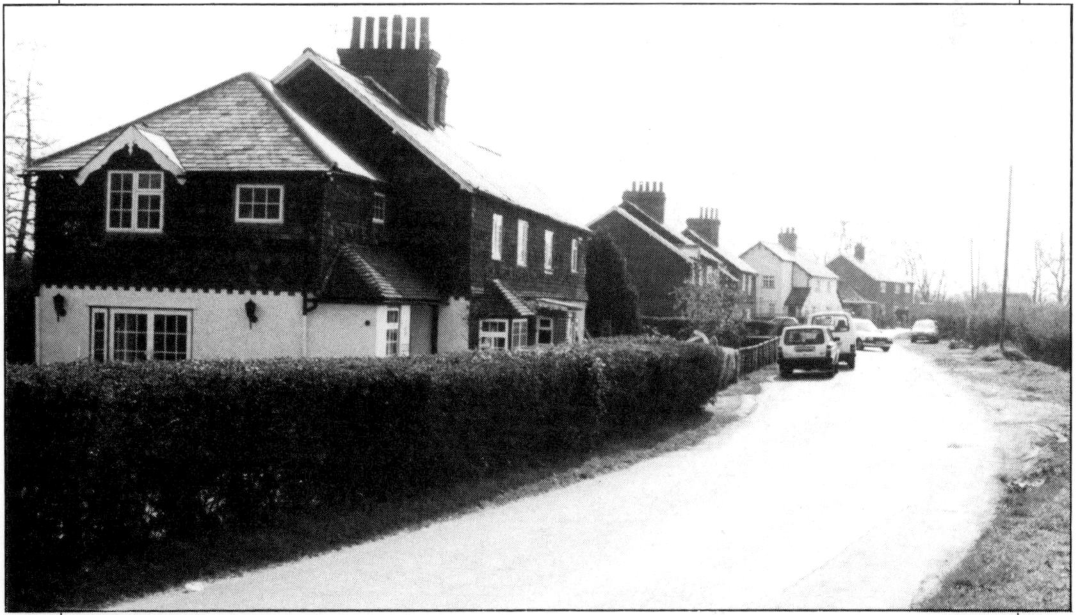

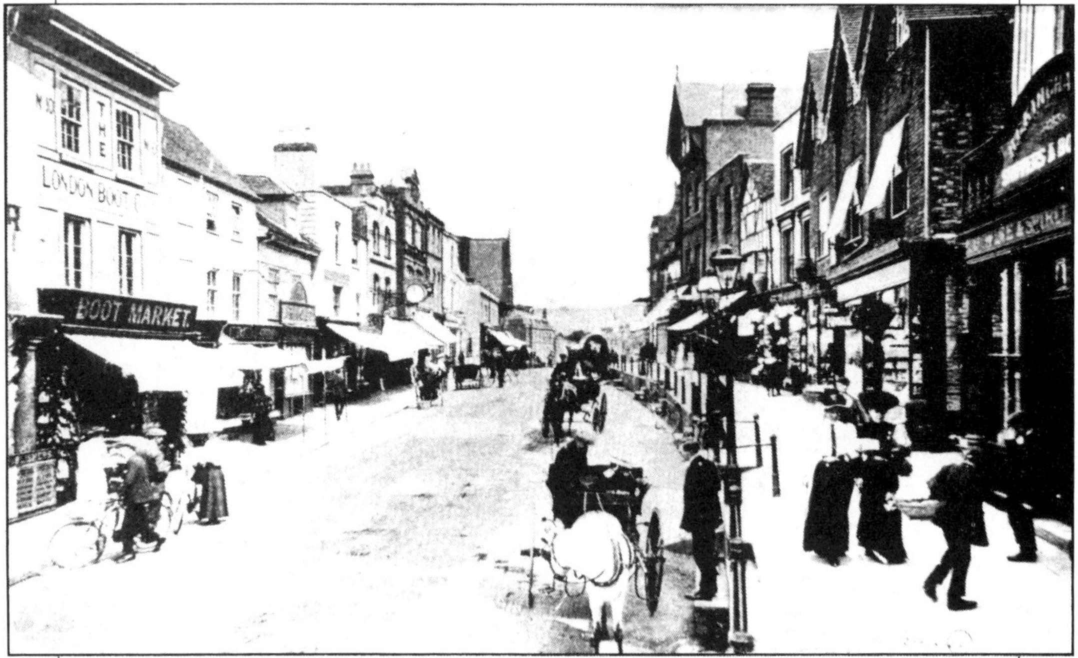

This view of Dorking High Street shows the contrast between the town in the early 1900s and today. Horse-drawn carriages have been replaced by cars and lorries. The London Boot Market and International stores have become the Linen shop and the Hearing Centre. The railings to the right of the pictures are identical as are many of the buildings. The layout of the street and its skyline appear to have changed little, although the pace of life seems to be much busier.

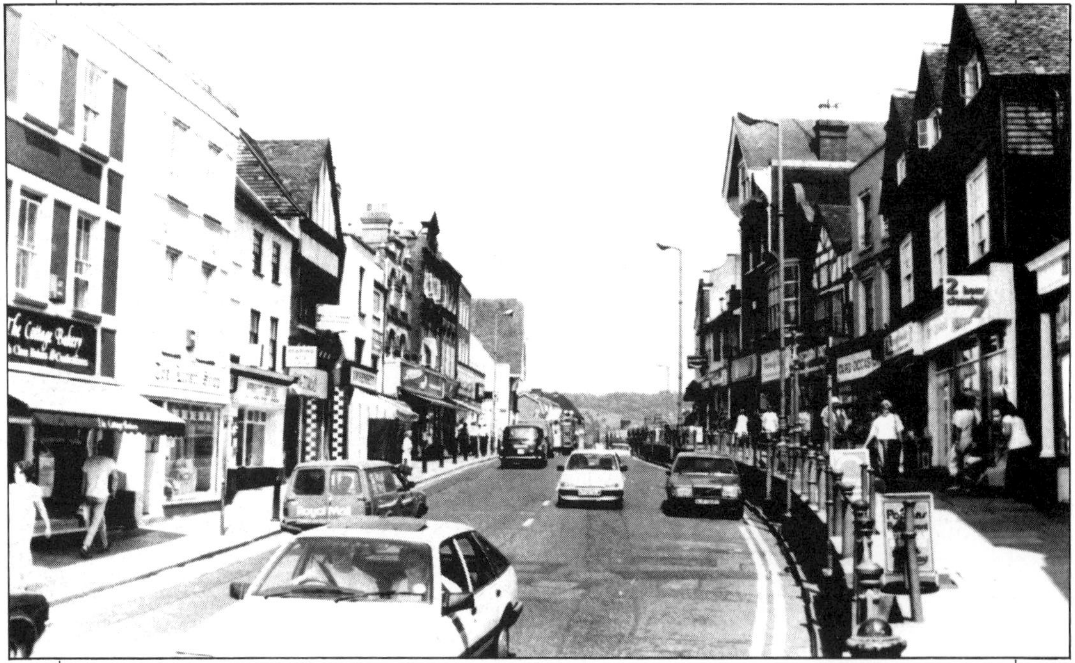

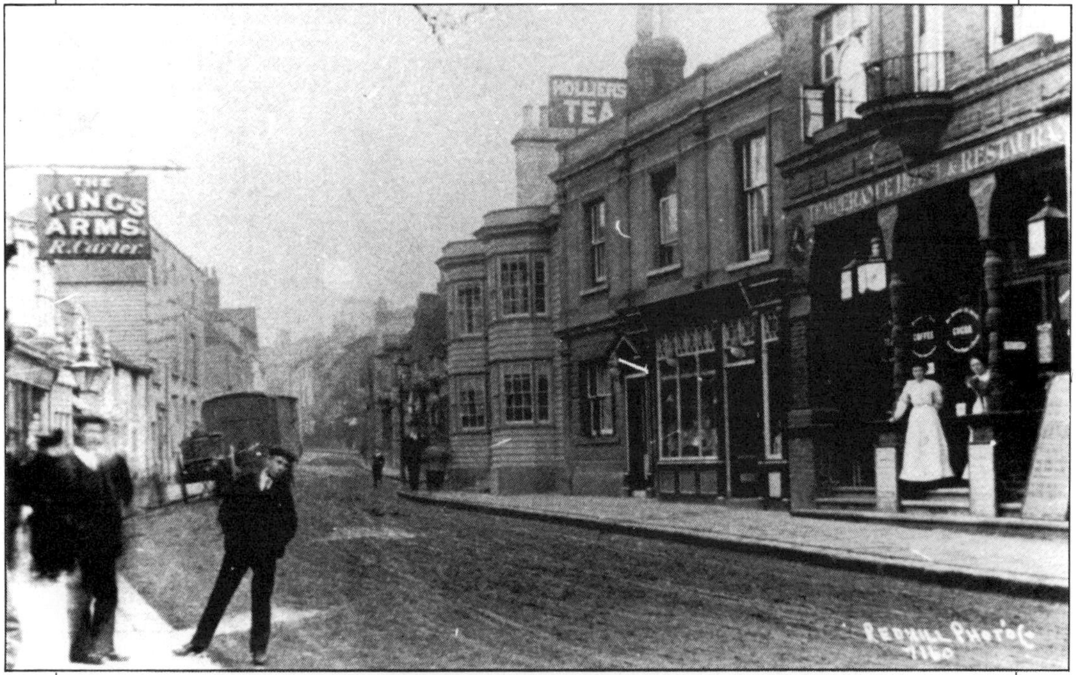

At one time, all the streets leading to the centre of Dorking town looked like West Street. But it alone has retained its appearance.

A century ago, there was a toll bar across the bottom of West Street, which then had an even greater variety of inns. On the left of the pictures can be seen the Kings Arms, which survives today along with the Old House at Home.

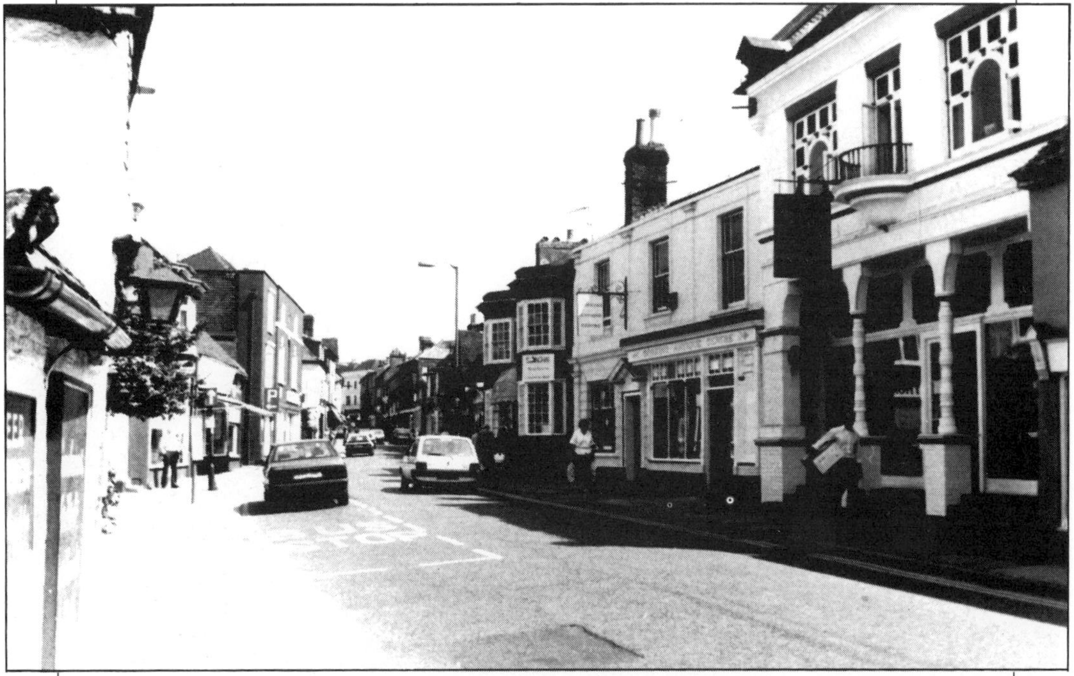

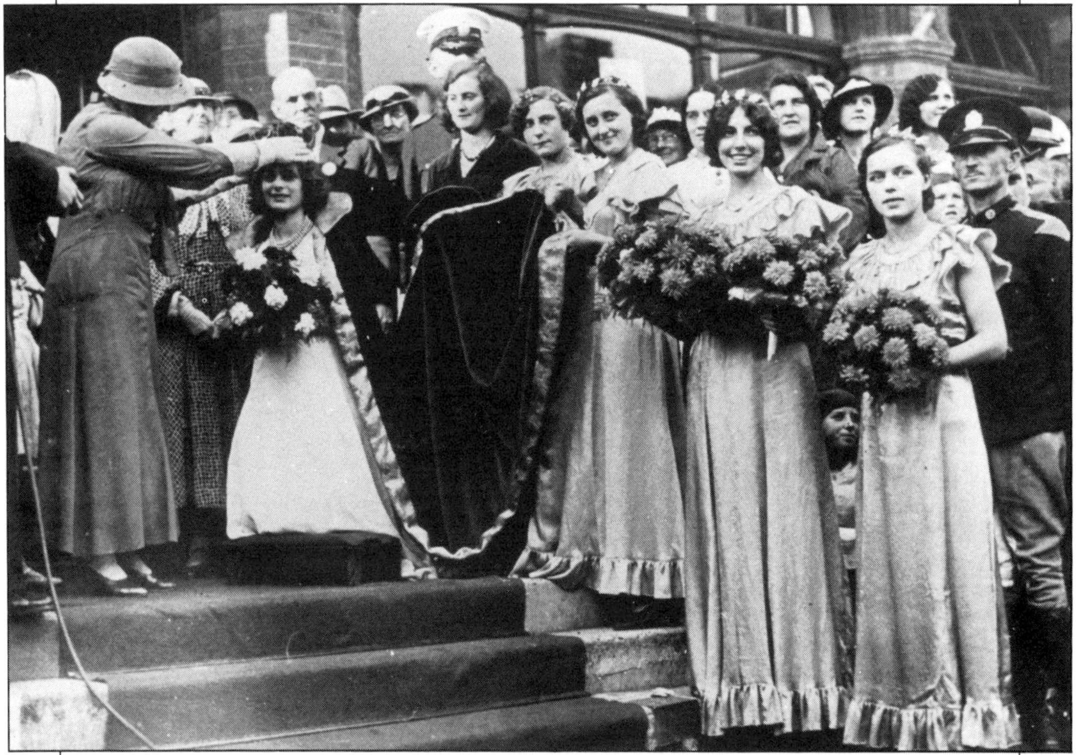

The carnival queen for Reigate at her crowning ceremony in the late 1930s.

The Sussex Arms public house in Station Road, Redhill and the neighbouring Celebrity Records shop have both disappeared. But Brewers and Sons, the decorators' merchants still trades near the same site opposite St Matthew's Church.

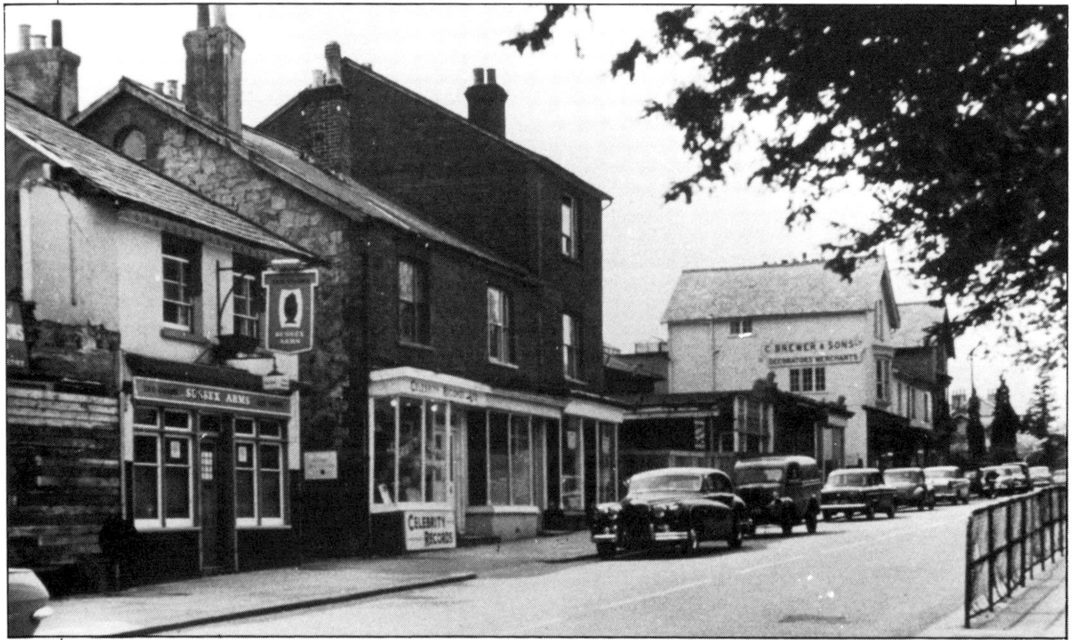

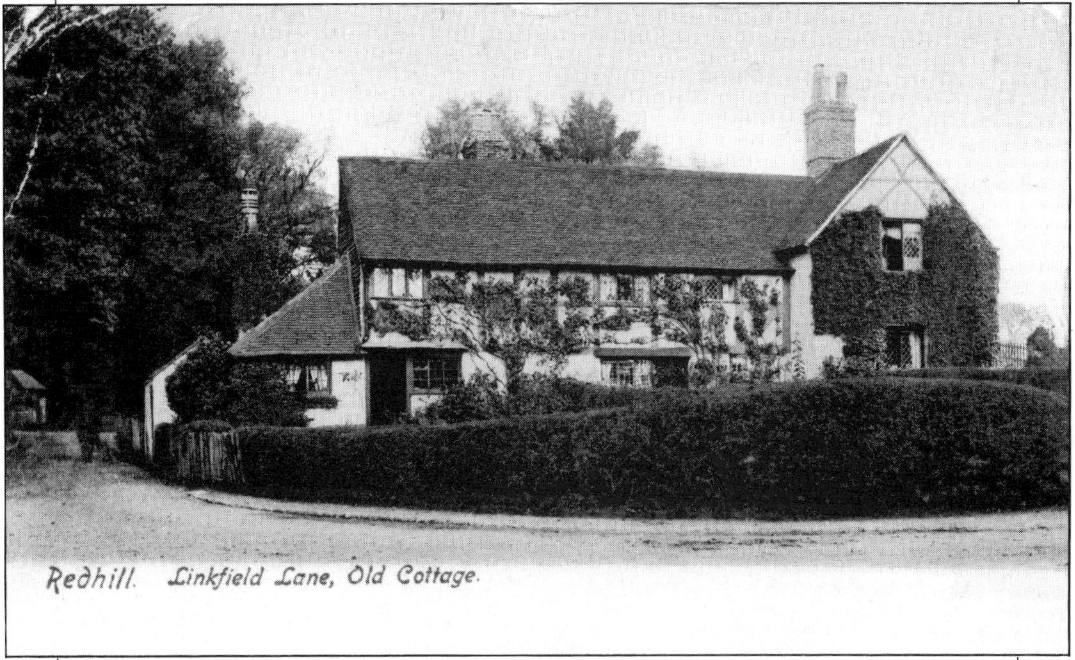

Some pockets of Redhill have survived the encroachment of modern development which has completely changed the old town centre. These old cottages at the foot of Batts Hill retain their old charm. They used to form part of the Linkfield Corner hamlet which stood on the original Brighton Road which is now Linkfield Lane and Linkfield Street. The hamlet's centre was The Red Lion pub, an old coaching inn next to today's Donyngs sports centre. Redhill's oldest pub is the White Lion.

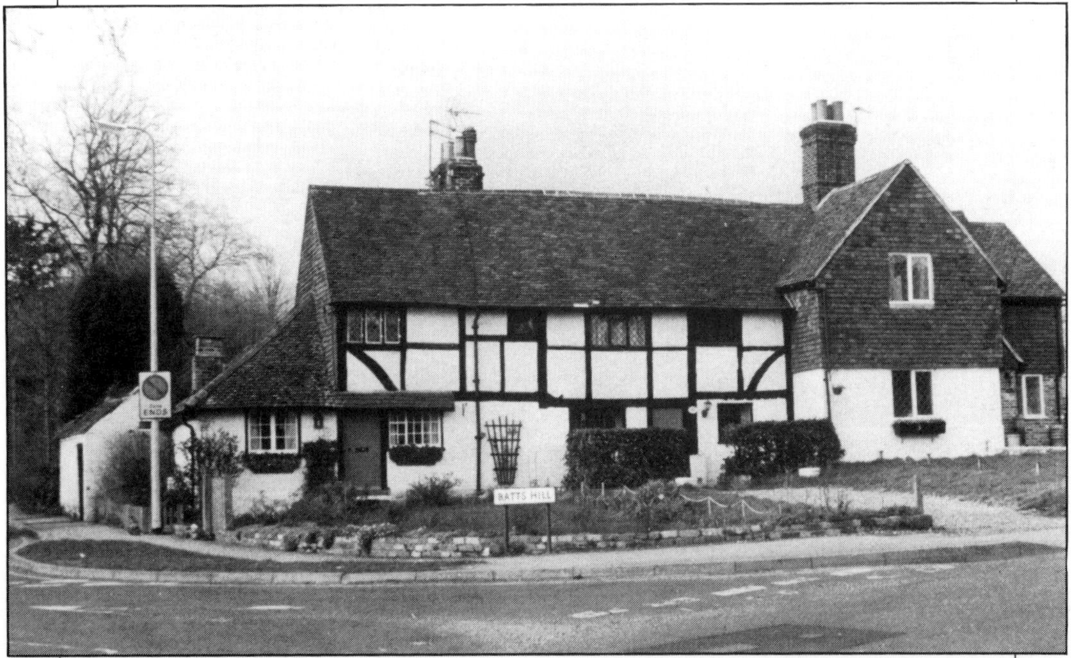

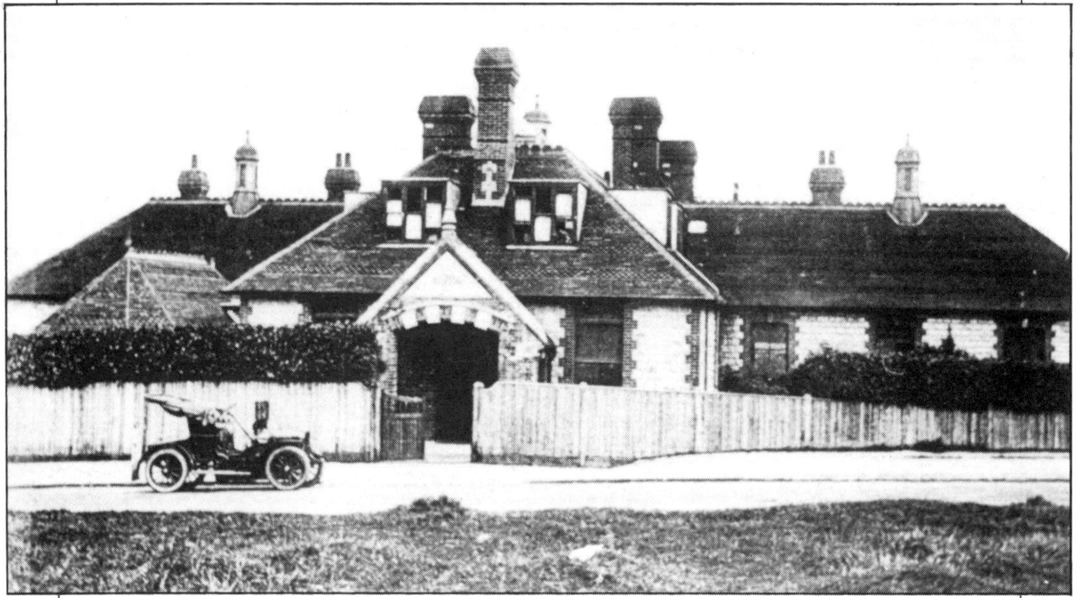

In the 1860s, small cottage hospitals sprang up to house villagers suffering from ailments who would benefit from regular medication, good food, a restful atmosphere, cleanliness and nursing.

The institutions were supported by voluntary contributions from local inhabitants, and one of the first in our area was opened in a pair of cottages in Albert North Road, Reigate, in September 1866.

By April 1867, the hospital was found to be too small and a site on White Post Hill, Redhill Common was purchased for the construction of a 16-bed cottage hospital. It was opened on June 2, 1871, and is pictured above in the early days of the motor car. The White Post Health Centre now occupies the site.

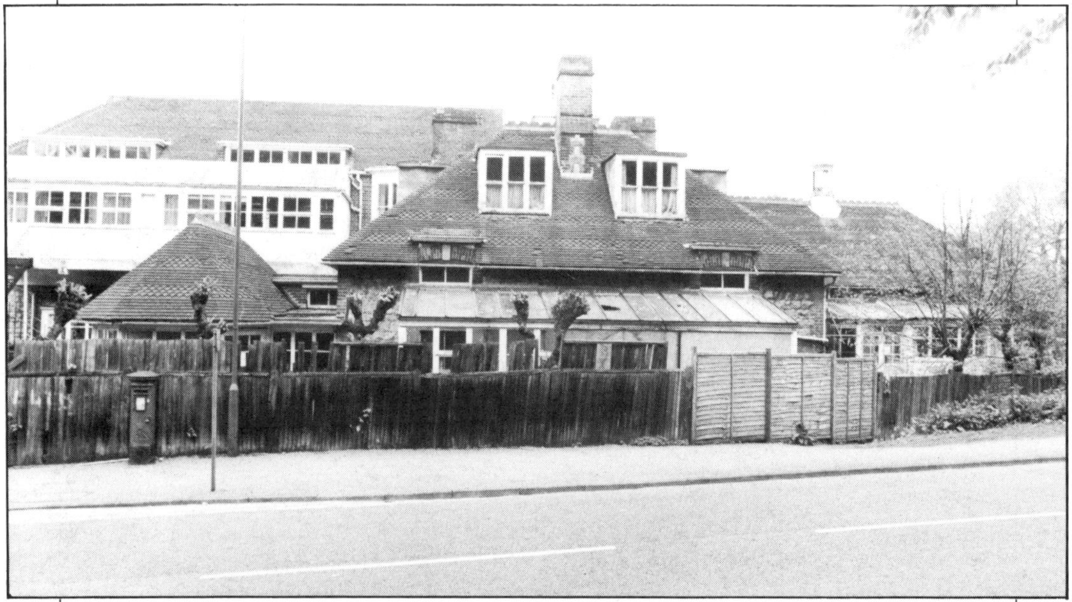

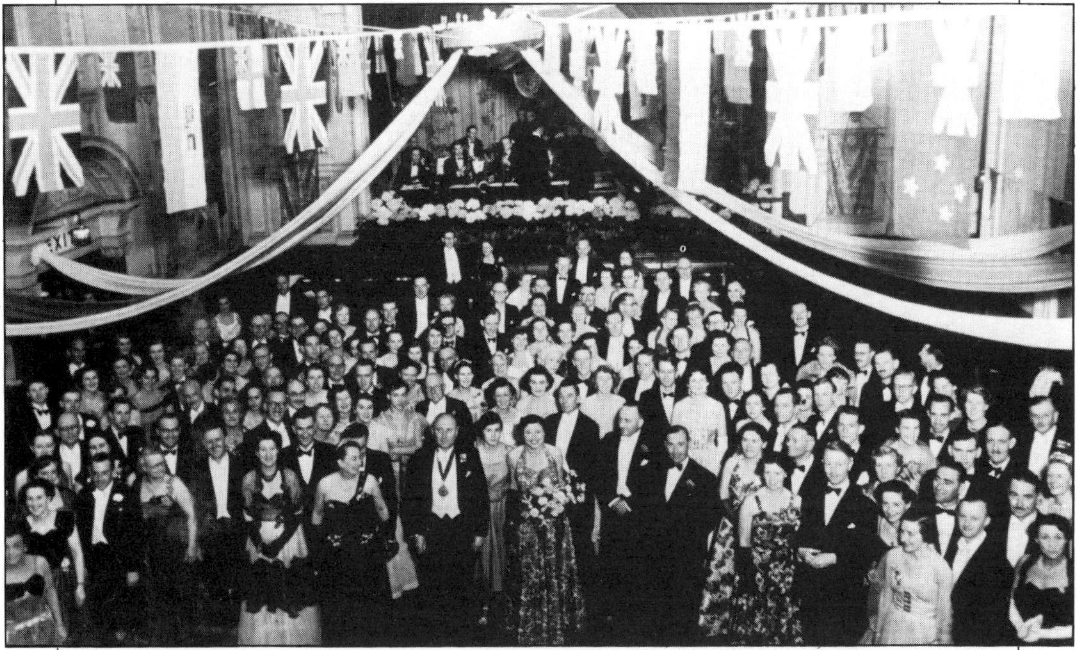

The old Market Hall in Redhill was bedecked with Union Jacks for the celebrations surrounding the crowning of Queen Elizabeth in 1953. This occasion was a coronation dance.

Earlswood Lakes continues to be a popular place for a Sunday afternoon stroll in summer. The boathouse is still open, but in new premises to those shown in this 1936 picture.

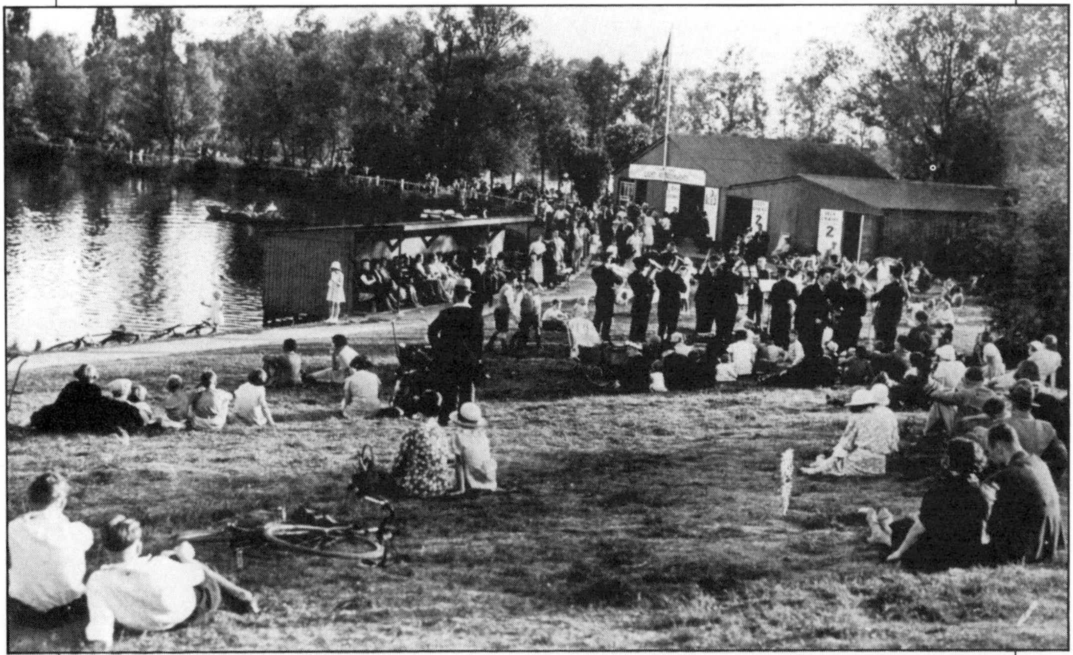

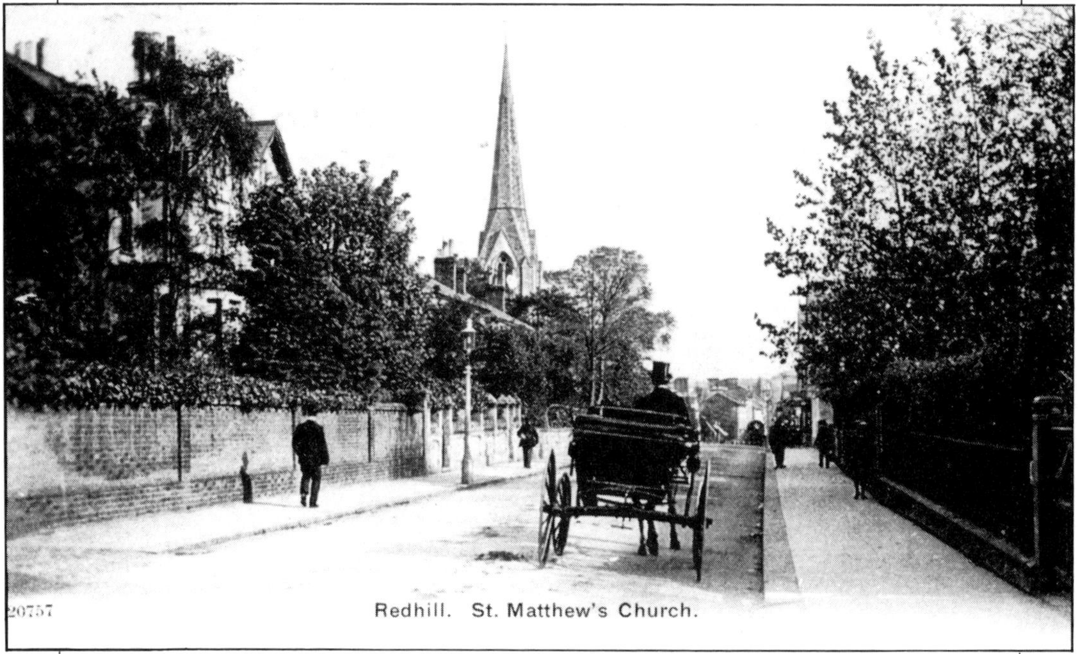

Few of the mid-Victorian houses alongside the A25 at Station Road, Redhill, now stand. One of the last to go was the home of retired dentist Mr Joel Winter. This kind gentleman, who never turned away a patient in agony, was brutally murdered inside his own home by two cruel travelling labourers in search of easy cash. Mrs Daisy French, the dentist's housekeeper was also badly beaten in the break-in during July 1988. She died only weeks later.

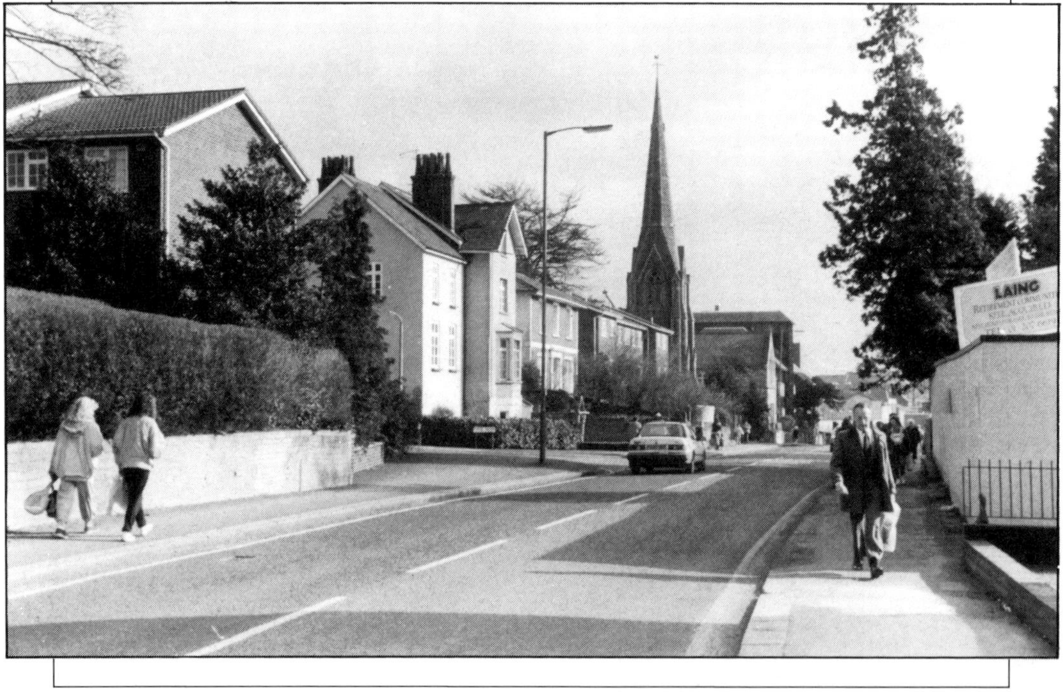

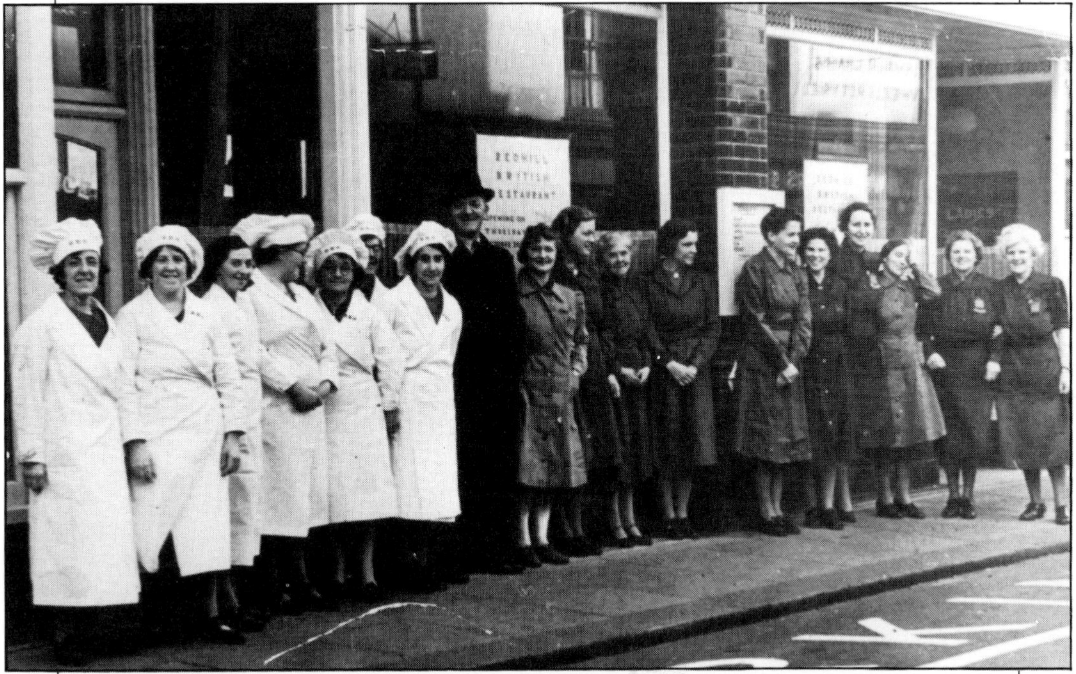

Staff of the British Restaurant in Cromwell Road, Redhill, where, in wartime, many cheap meals were provided.

Redhill High Street in the 1960s. On the left is The Towers public house, re-named Crocks in the 1980s, and further down the road S. C. Jennings, printers and stationers. The old family firm of Jennings still thrives in the town, but is now situated nearer to Chapel Road.

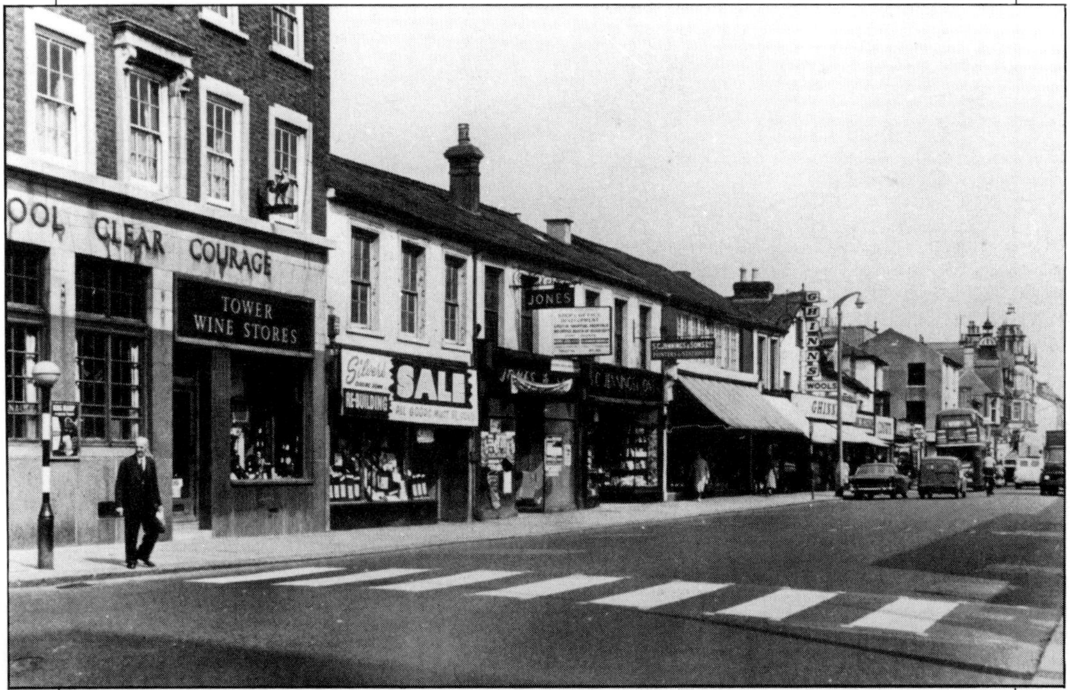

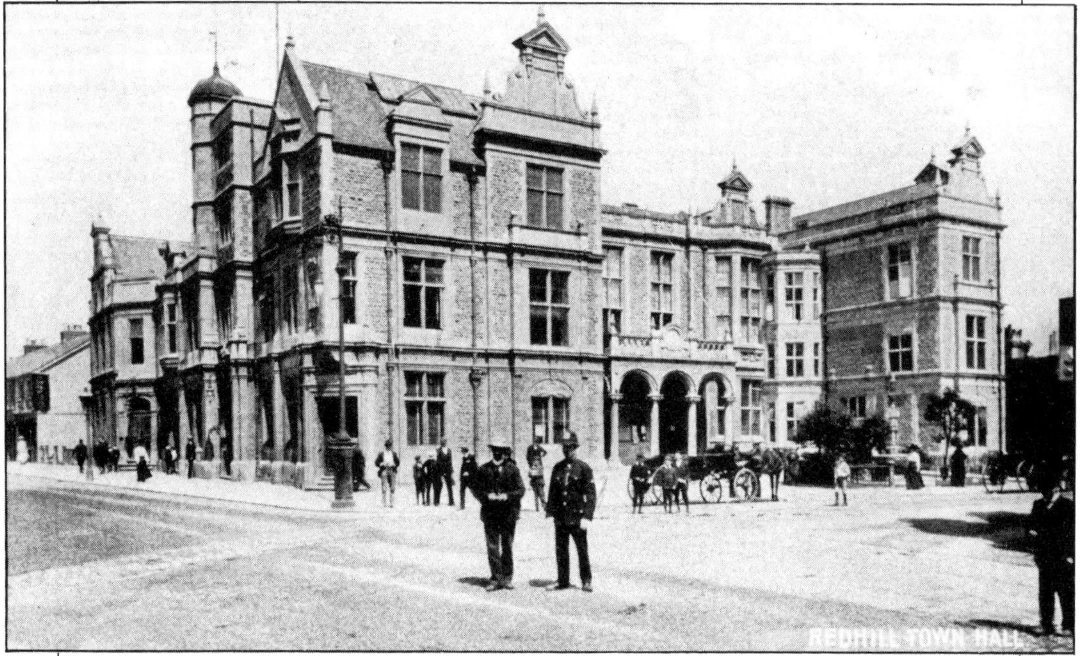

The old market hall in Redhill town centre was pulled down in the early 1980s after standing for well over 100 years. Redhill townsfolk have happy memories of social functions at the hall over the years. As well as operas and classical concerts, there were pop shows. In the early 1960s, the Rolling Stones, Freddie and the Dreamers and The Hollies played here.

Today, the hall has been replaced by the Warwick Quadrant development which houses a library, theatre and shops.

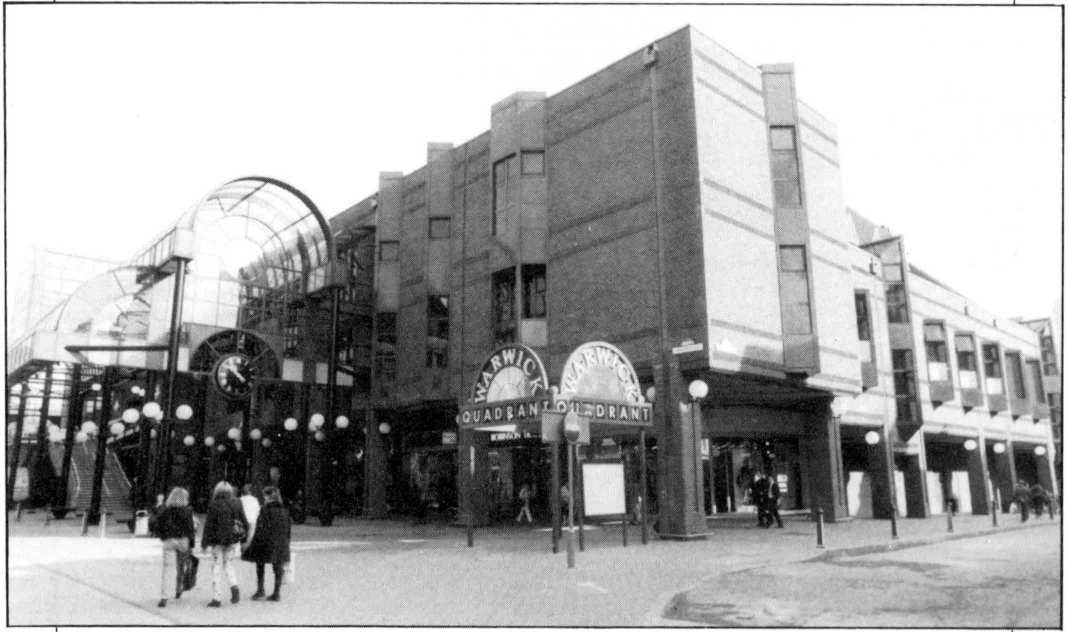

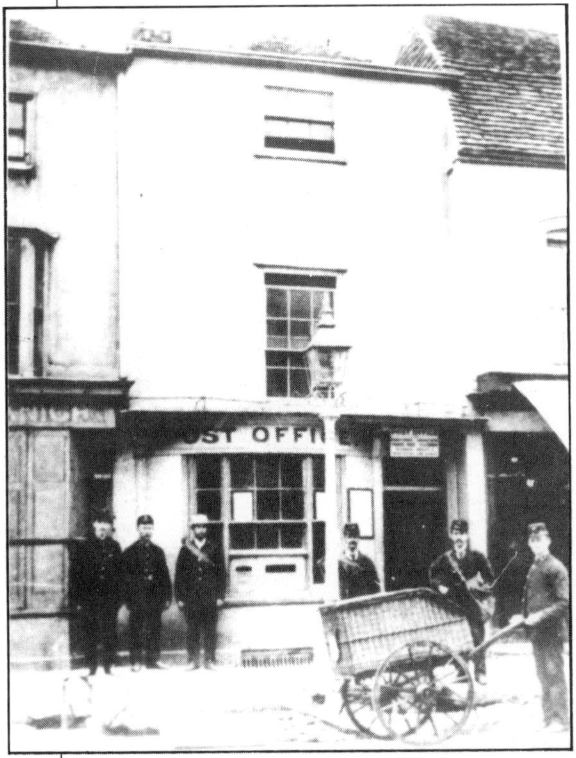

The old Reigate Post Office in the High Street which stood close to the old town hall. In modern times, the premises were occupied by Geoff Taylor, the florist's. Pushing the basket trolley was a Mr Knight who had a twin brother, also a postman. Wearing a trilby hat and carrying a satchel was a Mr Edwards, the general foreman, or carrier. He lived in Eversfield Road, Reigate, and eventually took over the main post office in Bell Street.

E. M. Ninnes, the blacksmiths, ironmongers and cycle makers pictured at the turn of the century in West Street, Reigate.

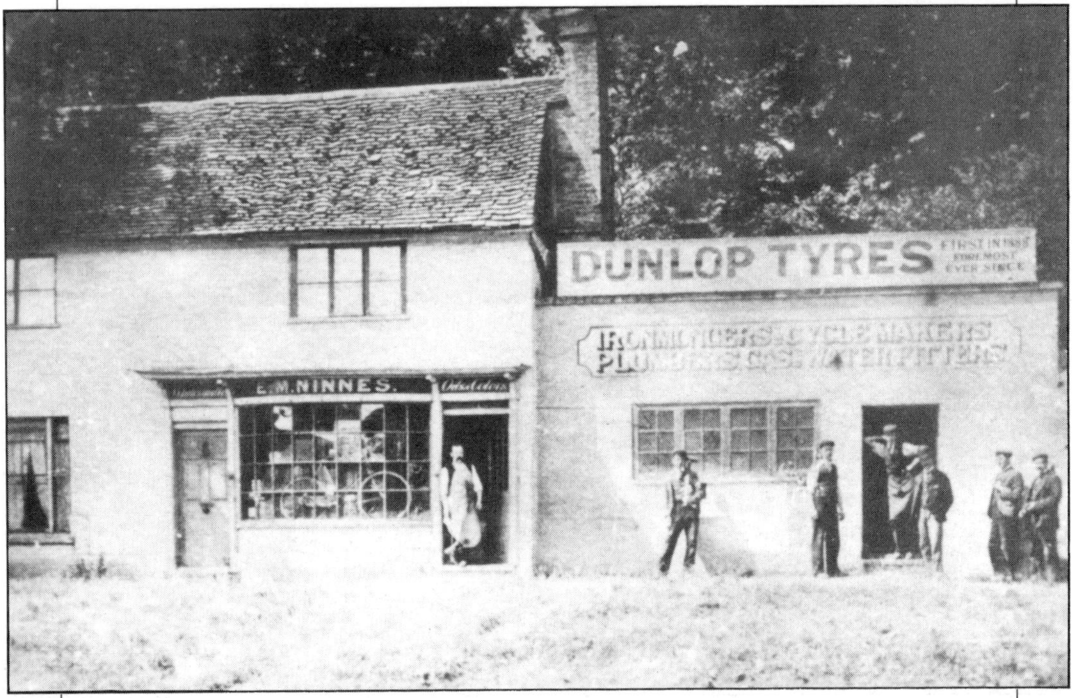

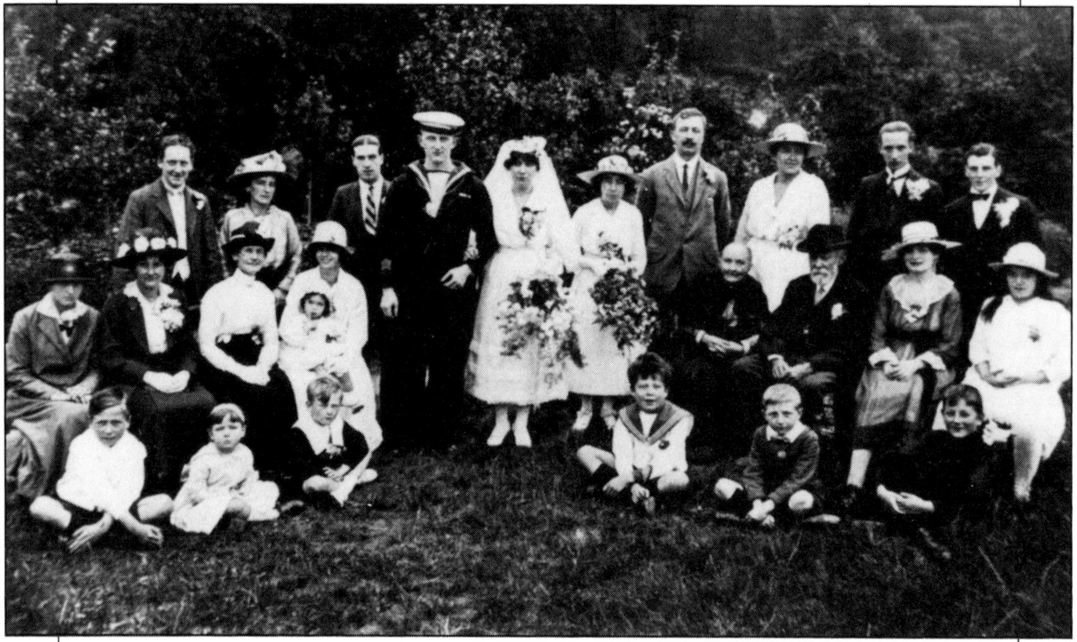

Between Reigate town and the community of South Park lies a cluster of cottages surrounded by fields of corn and wild poppies. This is known as Cabbage Stalk Town because, many years ago, the land was often covered with a carpet of rotting cabbage stalks. This picture shows a wedding reception at the hamlet in the 1920s.

BOROUGH OF REIGATE

ALERTS	893
INCIDENTS	184
HIGH EXPLOSIVE BOMBS	496
OIL BOMBS	18
INCENDIARY BOMBS ... ... (*approximately*)	5,847
FLYING BOMBS	17
SHELLS (*anti-aircraft*)	42
MACHINE GUN INCIDENT	1
MINES (*parachute*)	2
OTHER MISSILES	2

CIVILIAN CASUALTIES

KILLED AND DIED	50
INJURED	161

DAMAGE TO PROPERTY

HOUSES TOTALLY DESTROYED	115
DAMAGED	4,189

ADJOINING DISTRICTS

INCIDENTS.—Dorking and Horley Rural District, 266; Godstone Rural District, 684; Banstead Urban District, 204; Dorking Urban District, 123; Coulsdon and Purley Urban District, 700.

HIGH EXPLOSIVE BOMBS.—Dorking and Horley Rural District; 578; Godstone Rural District, 1,726; Banstead Urban District, 591' Dorking Urban District, 267; Coulsdon and Purley Urban District, 1,200.

FLYING BOMBS.—Dorking and Horley Rural District, 49; Godstone Rural District, 95; Banstead Urban District, 38; Dorking Urban District, 19; Coulsdon and Purley Urban District, 57.

KILLED.—Dorking and Horley Urban District, 6; Godstone Rural District, 25; Banstead Urban District, 15; Dorking Urban District, 25; Coulsdon and Purley Urban District, 98.

INJURED.—Dorking and Horley Urban District, 137; Godstone Rural District, 213; Banstead Urban District, 237; Dorking Urban District, 76; Coulsdon and Purley Urban District, 469.

In the Godstone Rural District 11 enemy aeroplanes were brought down. Oxted had more bombs than any other district in Surrey and during the Battle of Britain had 421 alerts. Blechingley Parish had 779 bombs, 37 oil bombs and 49 flying bombs. Godstone Rural District had 4 rockets.

How Reigate suffered in World War Two.

On the night of Monday June 19, 1944, the Reigate Borough suffered its heaviest blow in World War Two when a flying bomb devastated part of Earlswood.

Ten people and a baby were killed and a number of others injured. The flying bomb was heard approaching. Moments later, there was an outburst of gun fire from a battery to the south and east and, when this had ceased, the noise of the motor had gone. There was a swishing sound as the bomb dived to earth in the garden of a house at the corner of Earlsbrook Road and St John's Road.

The Surrey Mirror reported on the tragic event: "The terrific force of the explosion demolished houses and shattered others, burying the unfortunate residents in the debris of their ruined homes. That night, the rescue services and the medical units worked with unwearying energy, and billeting officers strove to lessen the cruel disaster which had befallen the district."

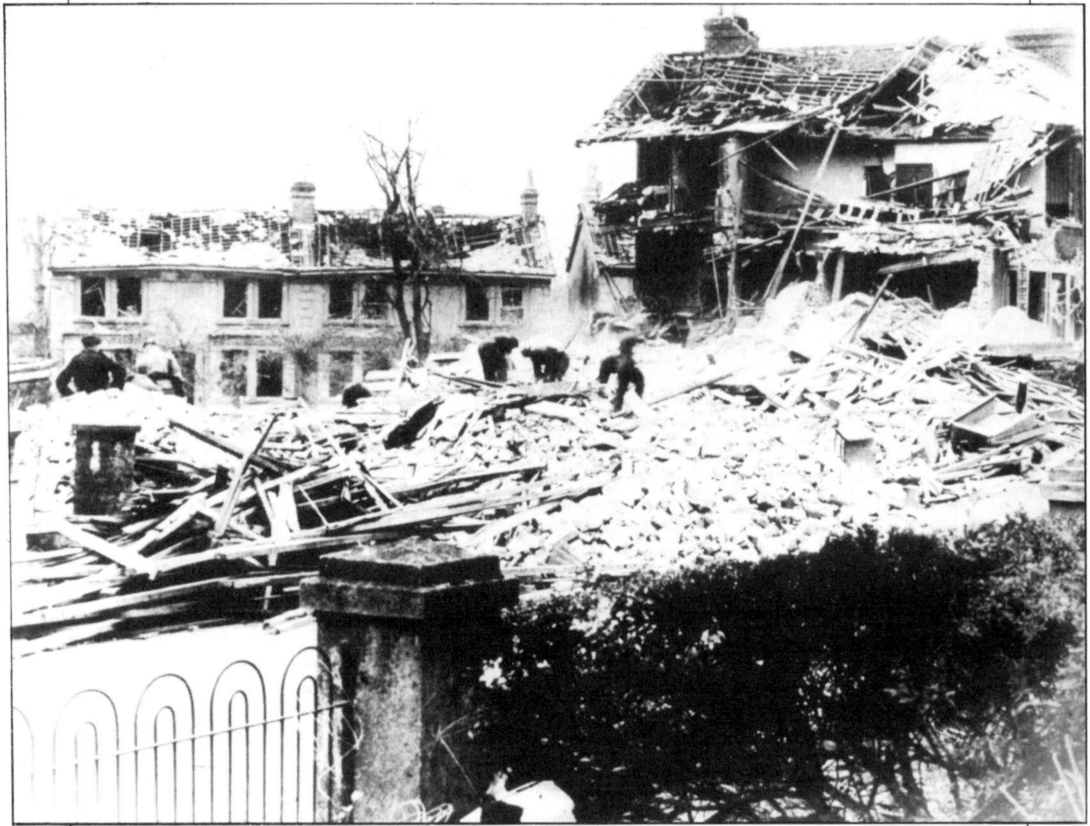

A flying bomb demolished several houses in Earlswood on June 16, 1944 and lives were lost.

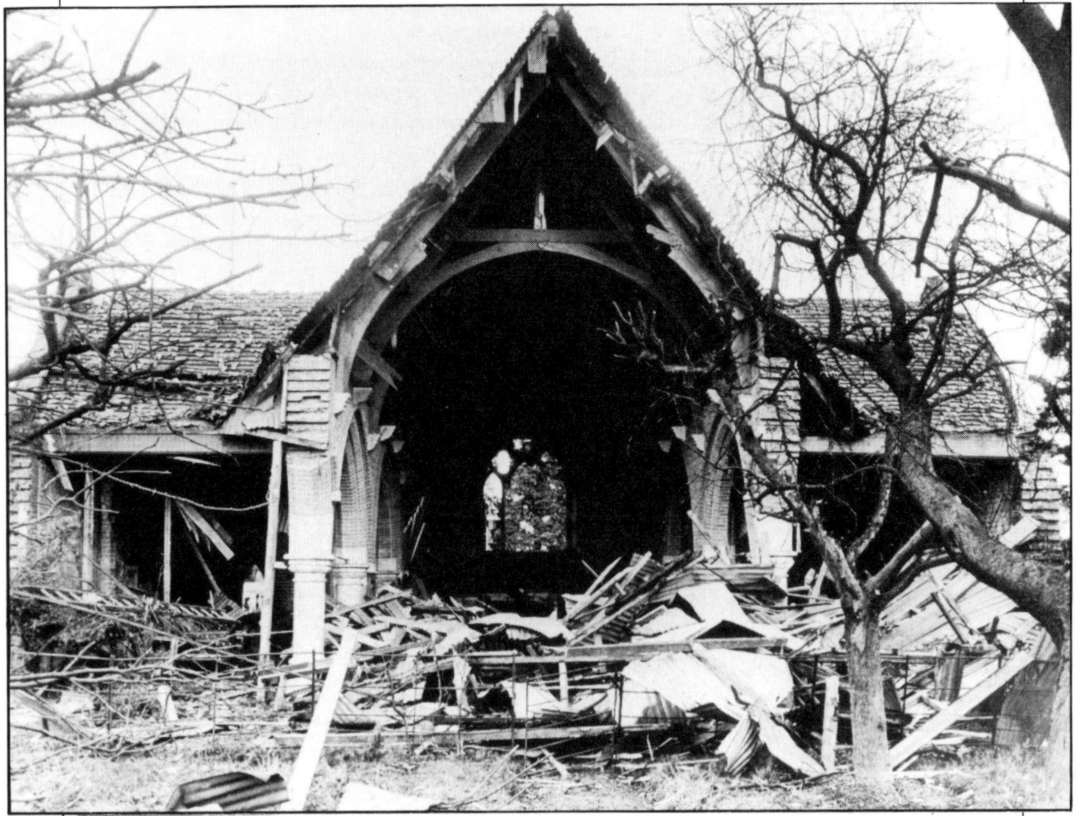

All Saints Church in Merstham was hit by a parachute mine on April 19, 1941. Next door to the church in Battlebridge Lane is Canada Hall, built speedily by Canadian forces as a token of thanks for the hospitality they received.

Caterham has two communities, one in the valley and the other on the hill. From the higher points, some of the best views in Surrey can be seen.

In the 1920s, at the bottom of the valley was the Harestone Valley Road which in those days just after the Great War was simply a chalk track. It was remembered for its deep grooves caused by the cartwheels and horses' hooves. Older residents recalled the lane being used chiefly by an old fellow who was a charcoal burner in the local woods known as The Scrubs.

At that time, there were far fewer houses than there are today in the busy town centres. Most of the roads were not made up and the rain which poured down from the North Downs turned them into quagmires.

The foot of Church Hill, on the corner of Stafford Road, was where a Doctor Davey resided. In Stafford Road there were few houses but then the road petered out into a track leading to Burntwood Lane.

In The Square could be found the fountain. Around this circular Victorian structure were drinking fountains. The increase in motor cars through the town led to its disappearance before the Second World War. For years traffic was directed by a dedicated RAF Scout.

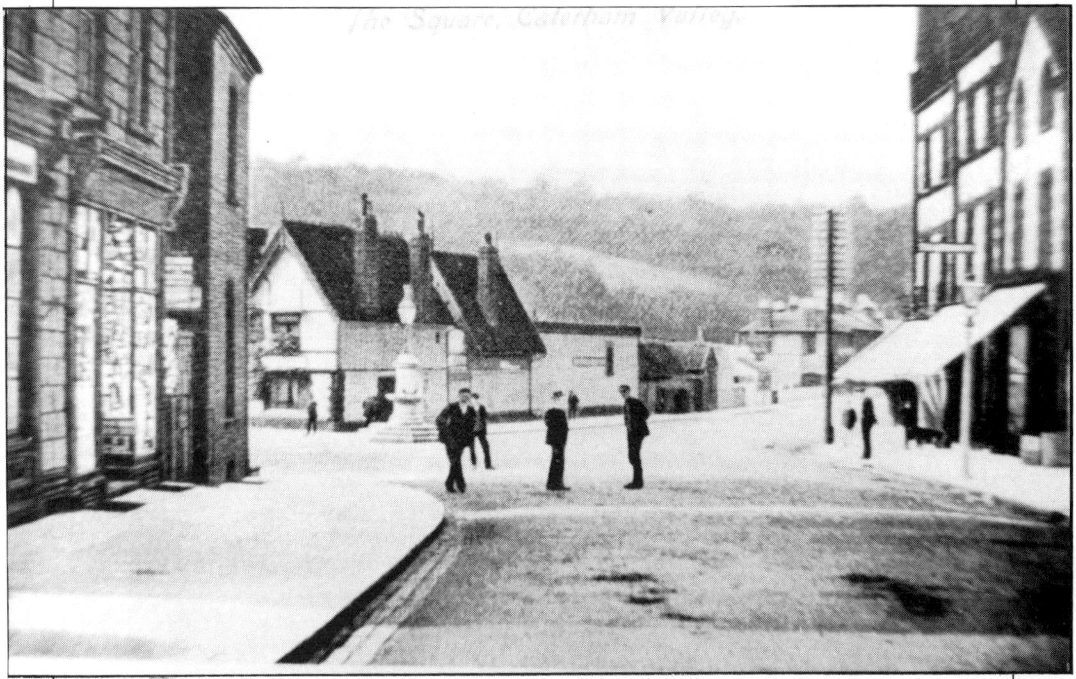

Caterham Square in the early 1900s.

Caterham as it is today.

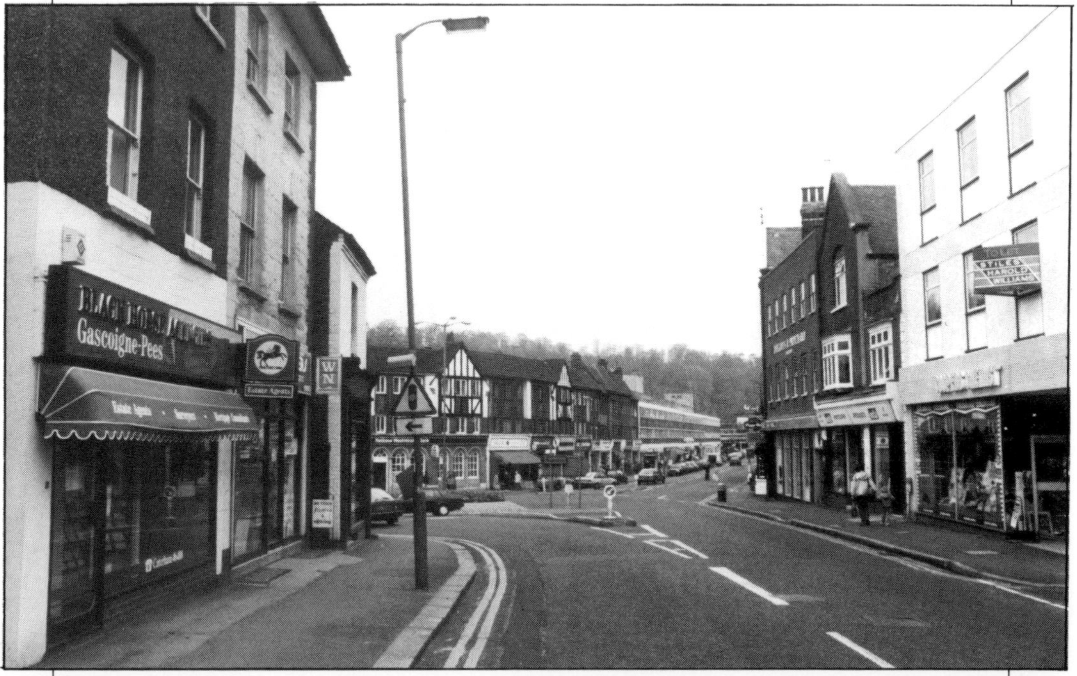

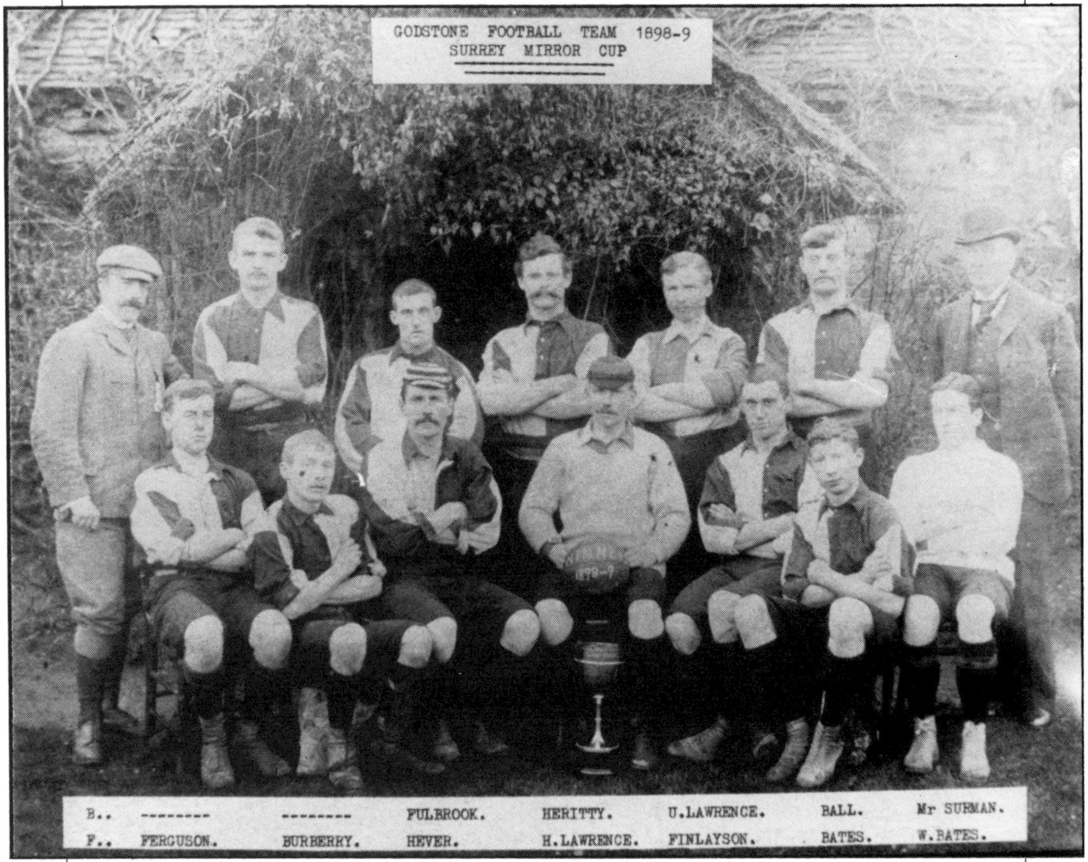

Winners of the *Surrey Mirror* Cup for football in 1898/9 were members of the Godstone football club. In the back row were —, —, Fulbrook, Heritty, U. Lawrence, Ball and Mr Surnam. The front row shows F. Ferguson, Burberry, Hever, H. Lawrence, Finlayson, Bates and W. Bates.

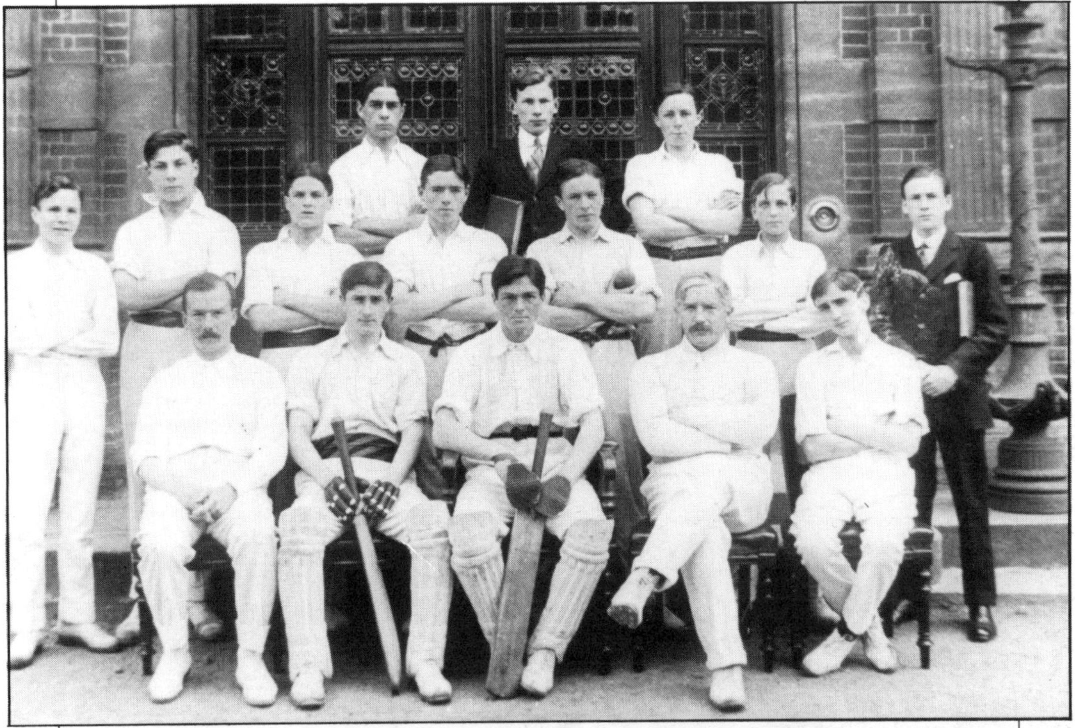

One of Caterham School's cricket teams in a picture taken more than half a century ago by the well-known Bunce Brothers. The lamp-posts which stood like sentinels outside the school doors were removed prior to 1948.

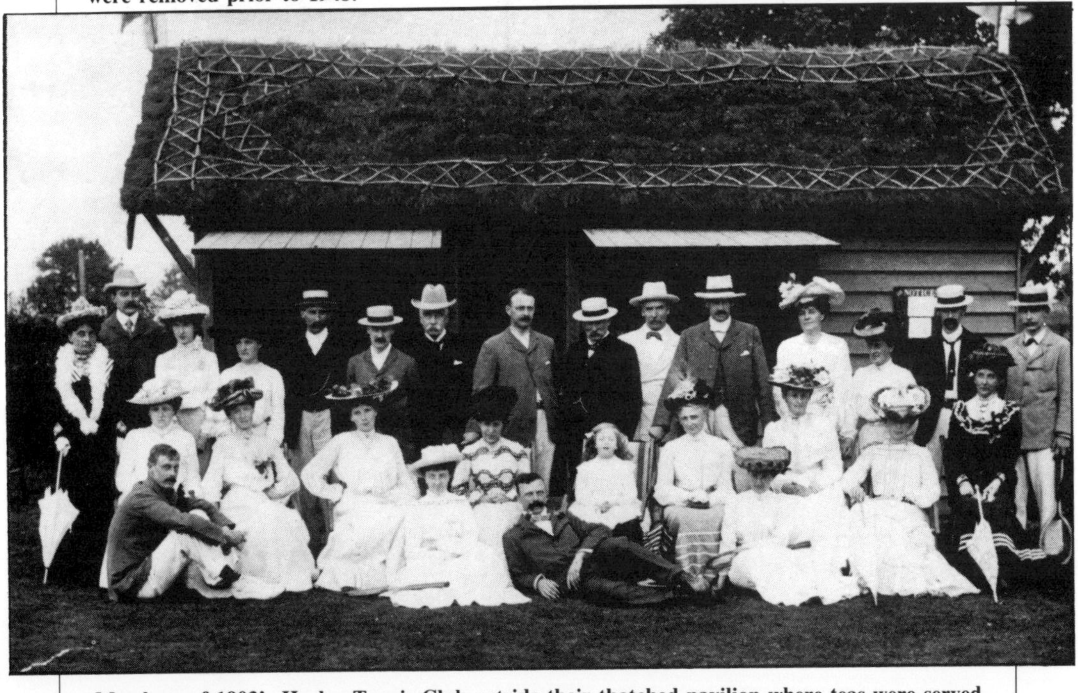

Members of 1903's Horley Tennis Club outside their thatched pavilion where teas were served.

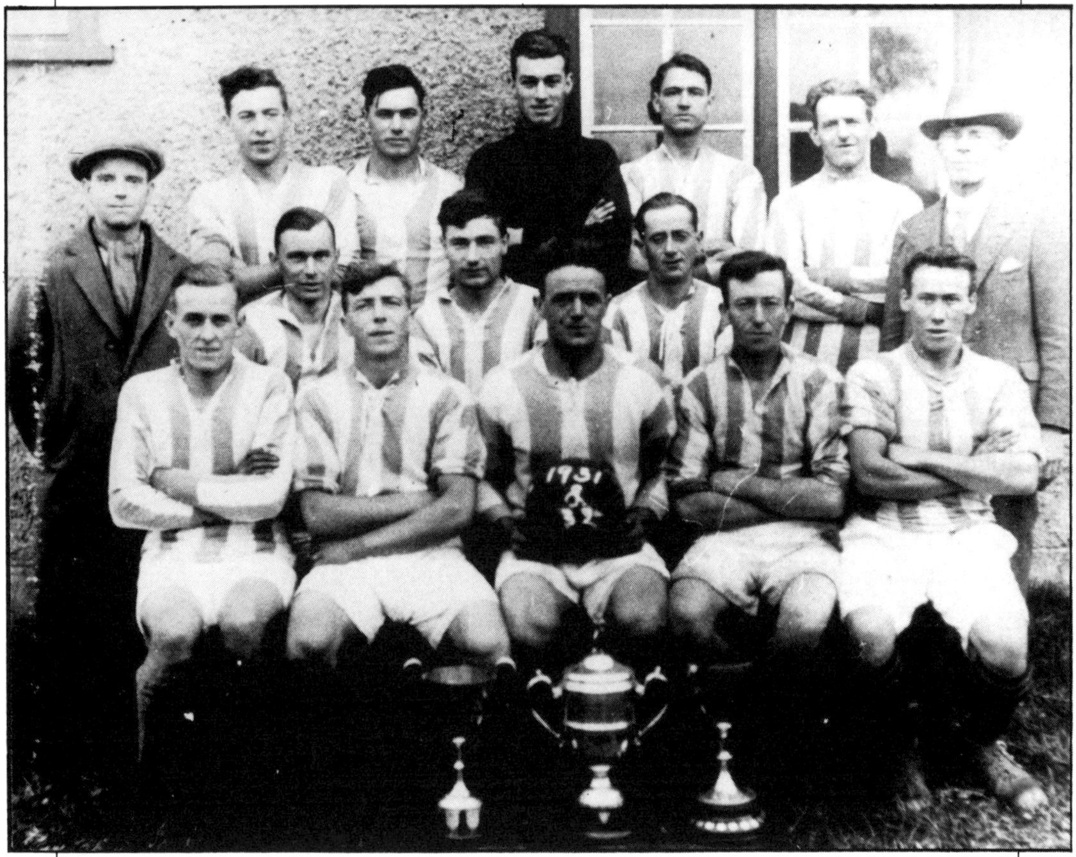

Godstone Football Club second XI, 1931–2.

Godstone Football Club second XI, 1931–2 who won the *Surrey Mirror* Cup, Charlwood Charity Cup and the Redhill League that season.

In the back row were G. Carey (linesman), E. Stevens, A. Butcher, E. Pooley, B. Simmons, C. Potter, J. J. Hoath (Hon. Secretary). The middle row shows W. H. Tharby, F. Smith, E. Burberry. The front row pictures A. A. Crowhurst, J. Blackman, W. Blackman (captain), A. Day and G. Hall.

In the Mirror Cup final against Pirbright, which they won 2 – 1 after a last minute goal, there was "tremendous excitement" at the Dorking ground on the Easter Monday. Spectators included the Rector of Godstone, the Rev. O. A. Hunt and Mr E. A. Wilson, Hon. Secretary of the Surrey County Football Association.

A *Surrey Mirror* report of the match stated: "The match provided a display of dogged, rather than brilliant football," and that "Godstone's forward play was without the dash and energy characteristic of this team." It blamed the absence of its "excellent centre forward, F. Smith" for this.

Godstone's first goal was by Day, made possible by "Crowhurst showing a rare burst of speed."

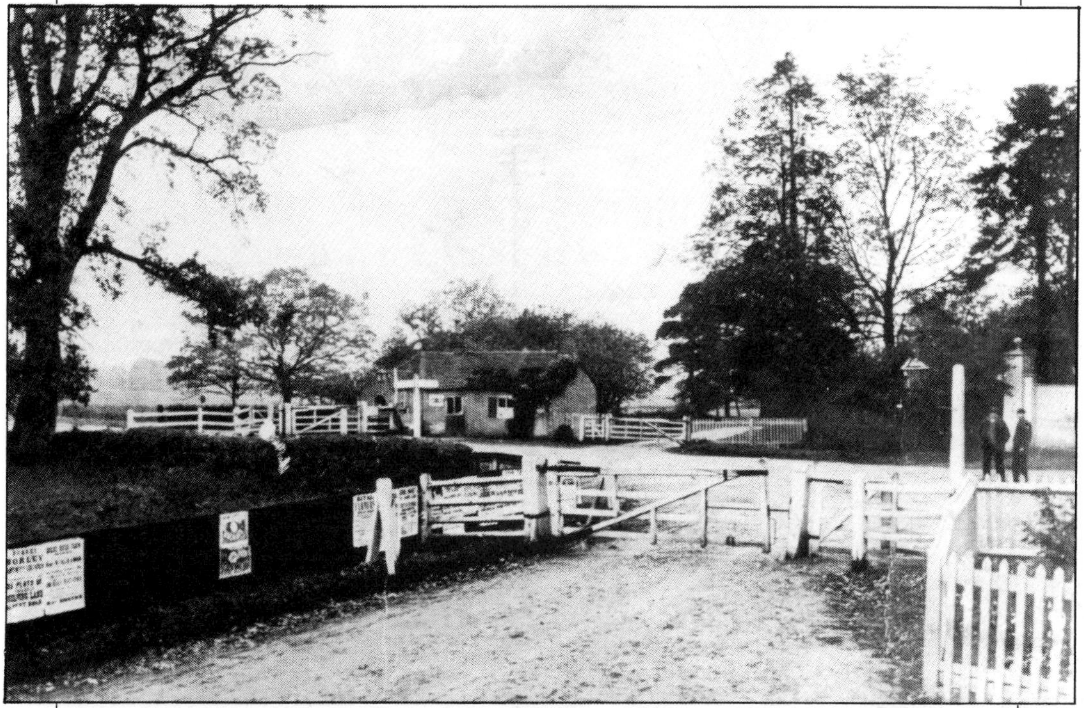

It is hard to believe that the busy shopping parade at Woodhatch was once a rural crossroads for horses and carriages. When the dirt tracks were improved, toll gates were set up like the ones here, next to The Angel pub.

Redhill High Street used to be full of small family shops. Over the years these have sadly disappeared, and their passing is still very much mourned by the older inhabitants of the town. Today the High Street is pedestrianised and the new Belfry shopping complex has opened.

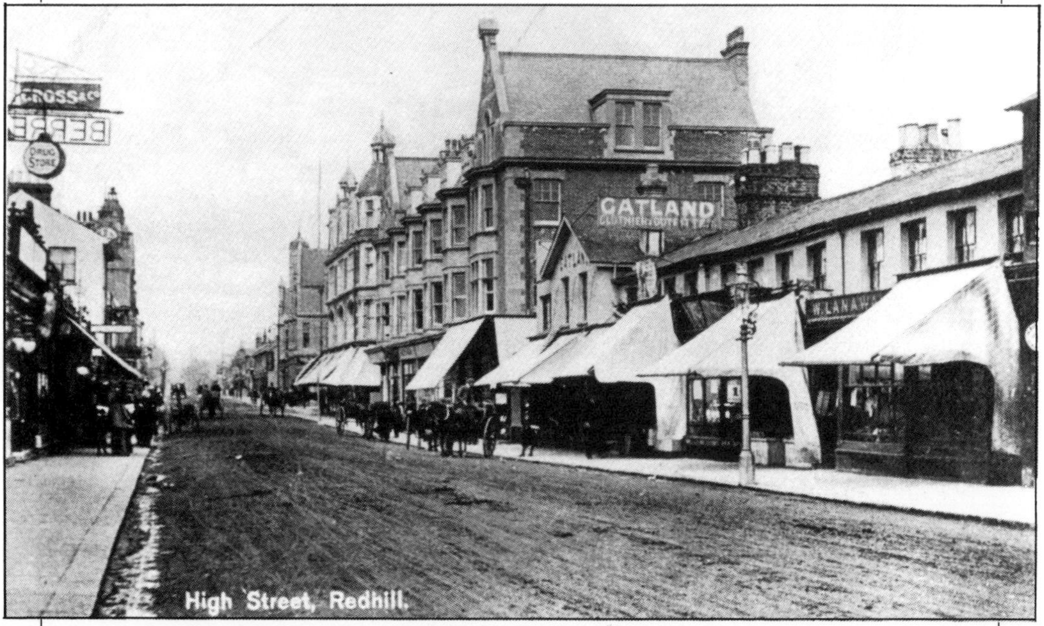

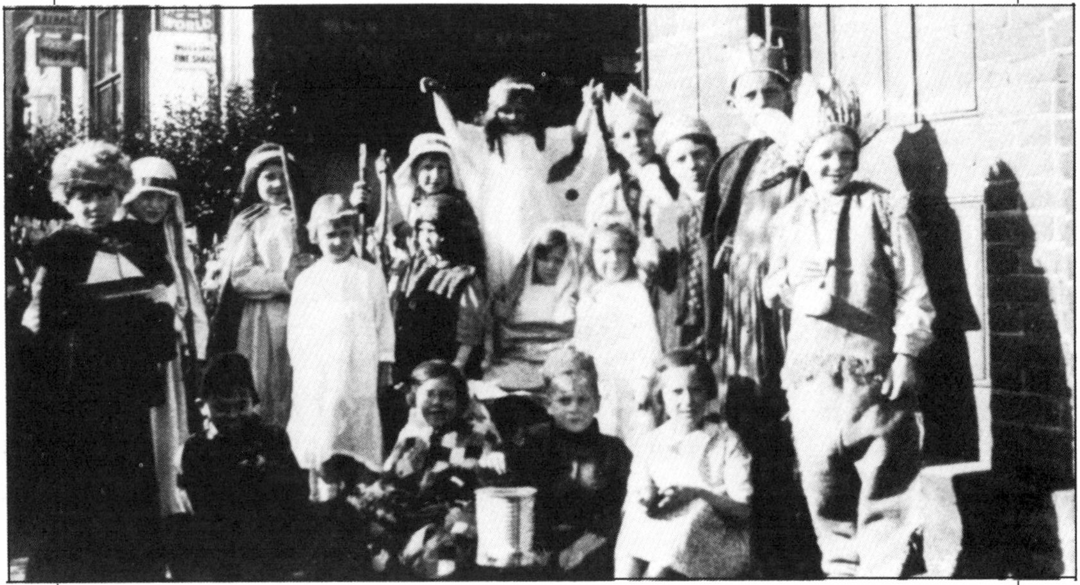

Characters in a play put on by the Meadvale Sunday School in bygone years. The newsagent's (top left) still operates from the same premises in Somerset Road, and the village has retained much of its individual character.

Wray Common was known in the 16th and 17th centuries as 'The Wray' and some 200 years earlier as Le Rie. The name is probably derived from the stream which rises on the common and meanders down into Reigate.

The old windmill's sails became dangerous around 1980 and had to be taken down; an act which led to a legal wrangle with the owners. In modern times, the base of the windmill has been used as a house, but with an extension to provide more room for the inhabitants.

The long grass, marshy areas and flowers on the common attract an assortment of butterflies in summer.

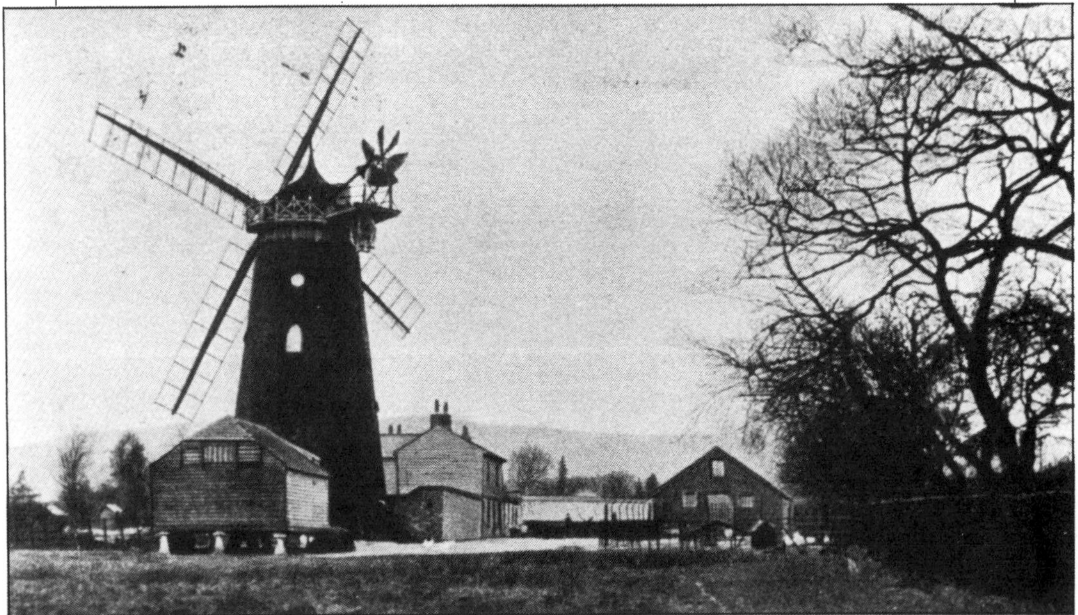

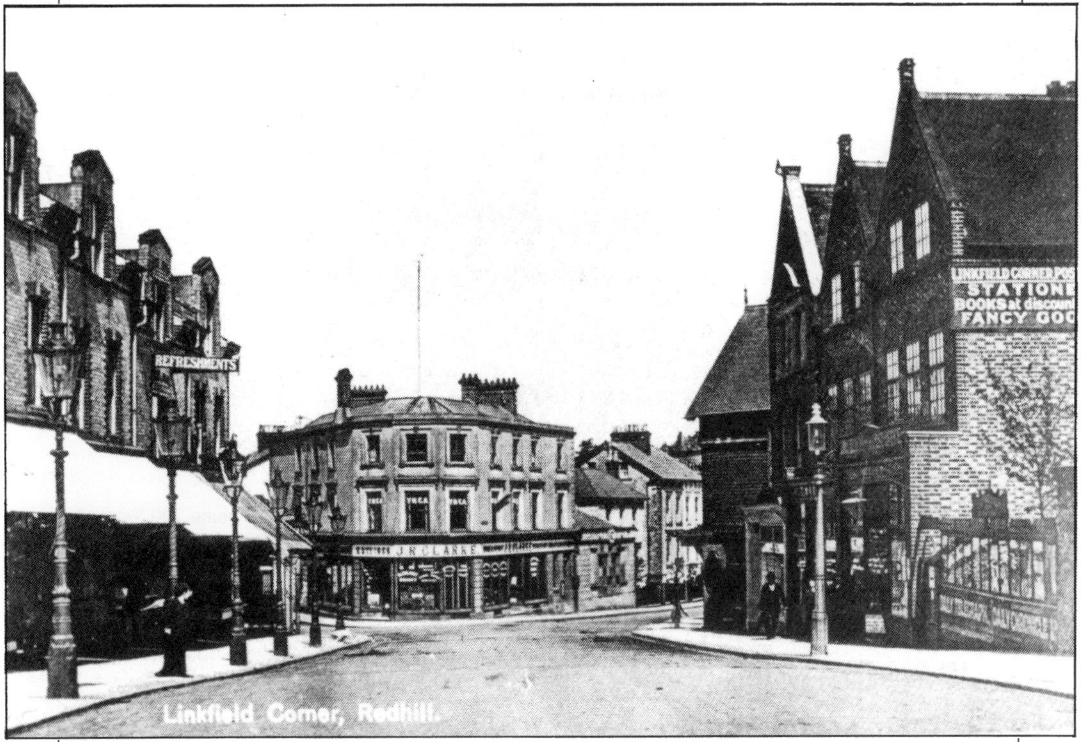

Linkfield Corner at Redhill has changed greatly in recent years, although the post office still operates from the same premises today.

The buildings in the centre of the picture have been demolished and replaced with a grassy roundabout containing flower beds.

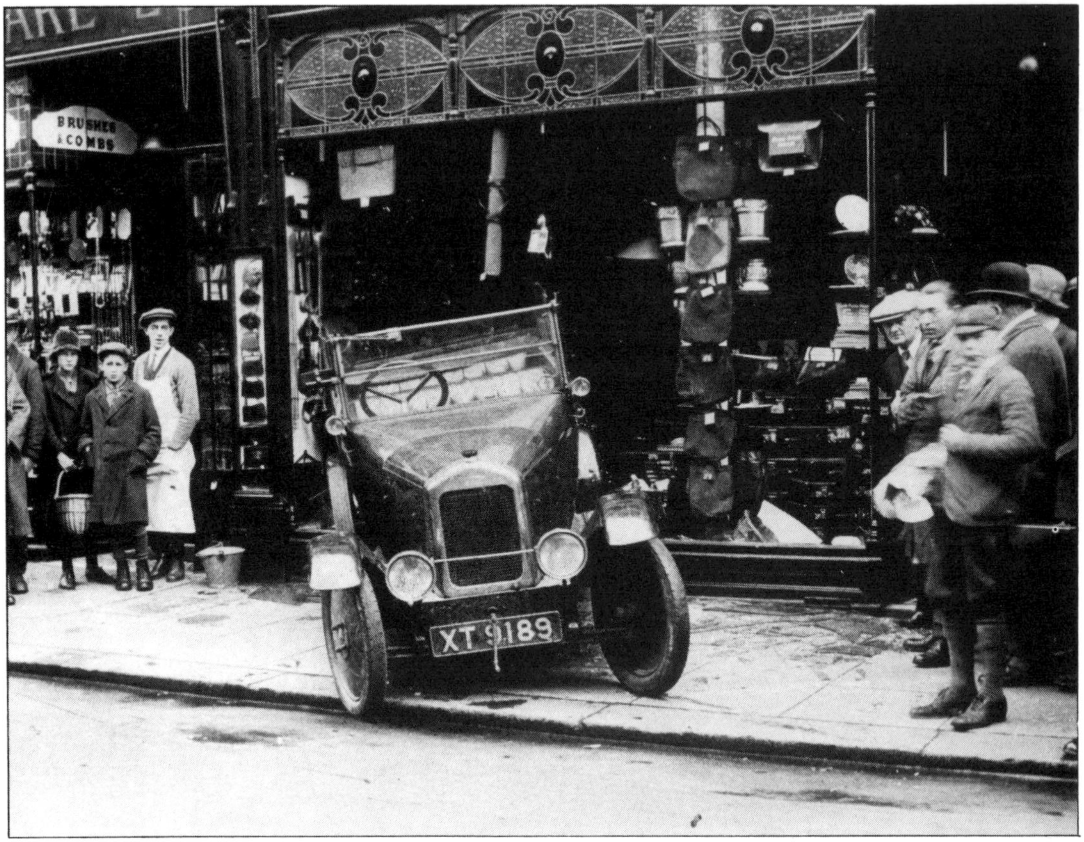

'I knew something like this would happen.' Photographer Jack Sales captured this picture of an accident involving a motor car which crashed into the shopfront of Hoares leather shop in Station Road, Redhill, in 1926.